West Country Cheesemakers

West Country Cheesemakers

Michael Raffael

BIRLINN

First published in 2006 by
Birlinn Ltd
West Newington House
10 Newington Road
Edinburgh EH9 1QS

www.birlinn.co.uk

ISBN10: 1 84158 507 6
ISBN13: 978 1 84158 507 9

British Library Cataloguing-in-Publication Data
A catalogue record for this book is available from the British Library

Edited by Alison Moss
Design by Andrew Sutterby

Printed and bound by Compass Press, China

Contents

Author's Acknowledgements

This book wouldn't have been conceivable ten years ago. It wouldn't have been possible without the help of the cheesemakers and cheesemongers who appear in it. I'd also like to thank Angie Coombes of Taste of Cornwall, Rita Ash who has taught cheesemaking in the West Country, to Dom Lane of West Country Farmhouse Cheesemakers, Mark Sharman for supplying photographs of the Sharpham Estate on pages 152 and 153, Lynher Dairy for photographs of Yarg, Neal's Yard for the photograph by Simon Tobias of its Covent Garden shop, Bray Leino for the cheese ironing picture in the prelims, Pat Robinson-Aldridge for her memories of James Aldridge and Jeremy Bowen of Paxton & Whitfield. Also I'd like to thank the editorial team of Alison Moss and Katy Charge for prompt and helpful guidance, with a special word for Holly and Jake for their boundless optimism.

Introduction

The story of cheesemaking in the west of England could legitimately start with early historical sources and work forwards from there – a manuscript of royal accounts, for instance, dating from 1170, that records Henry II's exchequer buying four tons of Somerset cheese at a cost of a farthing per pound.

This isn't, though, an academic work, so I'm going back a mere twenty years or so to a farm outside Taunton that used to make cheddar. Grant's was one of three farms that still made it without pasteurising the milk. The two others, Montgomery's in the shadow of Cadbury Castle and Keen's near Wincanton, have both outlasted it. What made it special for me was that it planted a benchmark in my head by which I would measure other cheddars. It wasn't particularly old, less than a year. The texture to my untutored palate was no better than something off a supermarket counter. On the other hand, its taste was unique, completely satisfying, and if I were to attempt to describe it at this distance in time, I'd be doing a disservice to its memory.

What it taught me was that there were two kinds of cheddar. The branded creamery version was made to a strict manufacturing standard that never altered except in the controlled degree of maturity. The farmhouse one, however, was unpredictable. It might be no better or even worse than something foisted onto the market at the rate of a thousand tonnes a week, but it could also rise above the ordinary, becoming something that justified the skill, the labour and the instinct that went into producing it, not to mention an intangible modicum of luck.

Grant's is no longer. Like about a dozen other farms that have ceased cheddar making in recent years – and in a decade there will be less still than there are now – it ran out of steam. Whether this was because a younger generation didn't wish to take on cheesemaking from their parents, or because the business wasn't making money, or because bureaucrats were carrying out a witch-hunt against raw milk products doesn't matter. What does, is that few farms with their own herds, except for the largest survivors, think that vertical integration, to borrow the jargon of business, works for them.

The slow, inevitable decline that has been continuing for 150 years can be shackled to a raft of different causes. Back in 1851, a New York State entrepreneur, Jesse Williams, founded the first commercial 'cheesery'. No British equivalent existed for another twenty years, but by then America had hundreds, mass-producing and exporting to the Old World. Often their merchandise was better than the irregular output of British farms. It was also cheaper.

In the south west of England, the counties spreading from Gloucestershire to the Dorset coast and along the Channel to the tip of Cornwall, cheese was a by-product, a safety valve for those weeks during the spring and summer when there was a surplus of milk. It was something all farmers with dairy cattle made. For the most part the task was carried out in a haphazard manner. How much was made depended on what was available. There was no scientific grasp of the invisible life inside the milk. The process was

dictated by custom, passed down through generations.

The small farming community of Cheddar on the fringe of the Mendip Hills might claim to have organised itself better than in other areas. Daniel Defoe, writing early in the 1700s, noted how farms and smallholdings operated a co-operative whereby milk was pooled so that large cheeses could be produced for sale at a premium to London, but their brand of collective farming had petered out long before the Industrial Revolution.

There was no way of knowing whether theirs was identical or even similar to the eponymous present-day cheese, because descriptions of the cheddaring technique of stacking fresh curd bricks along the sides of the vat after the whey has drained from them didn't exist until a century later.

Reliable cheap imports fed the growing urban population. They didn't usurp the reputation of the best farm cheddars. In Somerset during the 1890s a 'school', more of a research programme really, was established to study what distinguished an outstanding cheese from a mediocre or poor one: 'The formulating of a complete scheme of investigation of the science which underlies the existing practice of the best cheese-makers.' It also assessed the effects that different pasturages had upon the quality of the milk.

The main objective in setting up the school had been to examine the chemical problems associated with cheesemaking, on the assumption that controlling these would improve the product. However, its conclusions showed that what mattered as much, possibly more, was the influence of bacteria. It was true, researchers proved, that neighbouring pastures could produce milks of significantly different tastes that would be passed on for good or ill. It was also established that dirty, contaminated milk was the main culprit behind bad cheese. Bacteria made or marred: their presence either contributed positively to ripening or caused taints.

Ever since, food technologists have aimed at eradicating any bacteria that might prevent a cheese from being saleable. If by doing so beneficial bacteria are also destroyed, well, that's just unfortunate collateral damage.

Despite the efforts that had been spent encouraging farmers to produce better cheese, effectively giving them the knowledge to compete with the foreign factories, they faced a new disincentive. Until the Great War (1914–18), farms earned a little more from milk made into butter or cheese than they did from it in liquid form. That changed with the creation of the Milk Marketing Board that centralised milk distribution during the Depression years of the 1930s.

From that point, a farmer, regardless of the final purpose of his milk, was paid at two separate rates: a higher liquid milk rate and a lower manufacturing rate. There was a serious differential with liquid being paid more than twice as much. The ratio of the two depended on how much of the national output was going to liquid sales and how much to make cheese and butter. When the scheme was introduced, farmers received three-quarters of their payment at the higher, liquid price and the rest at the lower manufacturing one.

One might reasonably guess that milk production would rocket and cheesemaking fade out. Instead, the opposite occurred for two reasons. Bulk milk, of uneven hygienic purity, wasn't generally pasteurised. It might not taste good or it might be harbouring pathogenic bacteria. The public trusted it less than had been hoped. British cheese and butter factories improved and competed manfully against imports that remained high. Farms were encouraged to make less, but consumption was increasing.

The Second World War (1939–45) achieved what the market manipulation by government had failed to do. Due to food rationing, the cheese entitlement per week was set at one ounce per person. Farmhouse cheesemaking lapsed for the duration. In the aftermath, hundreds of small producers throughout the region found it easier to go with the flow, offload all their milk at a healthy price and scrap their vats.

The process of centralisation was bolstered by Britain joining the European Union. Its Common Agricultural Policy reinforced the subsidised payments dairy farmers enjoyed. Had the milk lake that this created been left undrained, farmers, who are no more altruistic than other social groups, would have continued producing ever more milk and, with no compelling cause to do so, the few who still produced cheese would eventually have stopped.

Introduced on 2 April 1984, milk quotas set the quantity of milk that a farmer could produce each year. The figure was fixed at 10 per cent below the previous year's level. It affected different farms at different rates, but it rewrote the rules of dairy

farming. Suddenly, individuals found themselves scrabbling about; searching for ways of recouping lost income that often represented the borderline between profit and loss. Pundits encouraged farmers to diversify. Among the few solutions that seemed viable, cheesemaking resurfaced.

The impact on cheddar continues to be felt, though not in the way that might have been anticipated. For a start, there are half the farmhouse cheddar makers that there were when quotas came in. The ethos of factory cheese and multiple retailing has been strong enough to elbow those that remain aside. But there is a cavalry charge of small (by comparison with a giant like Dairy Crest) dairies trying to sort out niches in which they may flourish. As a result there are farms that focus on organics, others that boast of low-fat cheeses. Having seen the word 'Cheddar' reduced to a generic, several others have covered

themselves with a European Protected Designation of Origin (PDO) wrapper that aspires to be a measure of superior quality and links their cheeses to a Somerset, Devon or Dorset provenance. Three makers who have resisted the temptation to pasteurise are grouped under the flag of the Italian-based Slow Food Movement.

Setting aside such arbitrary divisions that, in any case, overlap, it's possible to picture a cheddar pyramid where the base is represented by factory products. Somewhere near its top are a few large farms with their own dairy herds either making traditional rounds or block cheeses. Above them, at the summit, fewer than ten producers remain, each of which succeeds in making distinctive hand-crafted, world-class cheeses.

In their day, Gloucester cheeses had been highly regarded – and much copied. Wiltshire,

especially, shipped me-too equivalents (copycat cheeses) to the capital. Their making was studied in detail by an eighteenth-century agriculturalist, William Marshall: 'Gloucestershire has long been celebrated for its excellency in the art: and where shall we study an art with so much propriety as in the place where it excels?'

Marshall's systematic observation of the dairy proves not only how close the ancestral Single and Double Gloucesters were to those made nowadays by Charles Martell or Diana Smart but also how distinct they were from cheddar.

Considering their reputation – and size, normally eight to ten pounds and shaped like a grindstone – it's surprising that the Gloucesters failed to compete more stolidly against cheddar. As recently as the 1940s, André Simon, author of an encyclopaedia of gastronomy, enthused: 'The

tiniest morsel is pregnant with savour, nor does a greedier mouthful disappoint or cloy the palate'. Writing at a time of food rationing after the Second World War, he was defending a cheese that was already in danger of extinction, like Suffolk, Banbury, Oxford, Dorset Blue Vinny and a blue Wiltshire cheese known (confusingly) as 'Truckle'. In fact, if one discounts industrially made Double Gloucester, it probably did die out – as did Caerphilly making in Wales – before a few modern British cheesemakers revived it.

Vanishing or vanished traditional cheeses were a warning about the changing shape of agriculture. In Somerset, for instance, 30,000 acres of apple orchards have been ploughed up since the 1950s because farm labourers who had received free cider as a job perk were being made redundant. Those who remained in work preferred extra cash to 'scrumpy'. No food item that had been part of

the warp and weft of rural life was indispensable. If that sounds like a lament for some Golden Age when country folk only ate wholesome victuals, it isn't meant to be. Commodities such as cheese were picked off by the manufacturing industry because they weren't generally good enough to survive, just as corner-shop groceries were mopped up by bigger and better supermarkets.

The trouble was that the standard factory Gloucester, Cheddar and Caerphilly had less going for them than the better or best of what was being done in farmhouse dairies. Mass-production mops up the dross and the mediocre, but also threatens what's worthwhile or outstanding.

It would be wrong to treat the current burst of interest in hand-crafted cheeses as a revival because it's quite unlike anything that has been before it. Individuals farm buffaloes imported from Romania to make mozzarella. Artisans with no

livestock of their own buy goats' milk from herds several hundred strong. The most highly regarded accolade for cheddar, arguably, is handed out by the Italian Slow Food Movement. Curworthy was created by a trade magazine, *Farmers Weekly*, to entertain its readers. When a cheesemaker describes his product as being like Gouda or Manchego, he expects to be understood. In this still tiny pond of heterogeneous wares, devised by equally individual personalities with unlikely backgrounds, the motives for undertaking a labour-intensive craft for limited financial gain are equally diverse.

Robin Congdon, making Beenleigh Blue in the South Hams, originally worked in a bank. His neighbour, Mark Sharman on the Sharpham estate, was a mining engineer. Charles Martell, of Stinking Bishop fame, is a conservationist who studied zoology. Mary Holbrook, a pioneer of goats' and sheep's milk cheese, was a Bath museum curator.

Chris Moody of Rosary, another goat person, was an immunologist in a Southampton hospital. Their stories are all covered in Part One of this book.

Piecing together the disparate elements of place, product and personality isn't like interlocking the fretwork of a jigsaw puzzle. Bits may fit together, but not neatly. There is no homogenous image for the West Country as there might be for, say, Normandy. The concept of a regional gastronomic identity has never been cultivated in England. It's foreign. Attempts at inventing it have failed because there's a tacit realisation that it could never be more than a useful marketing gambit.

Instead, it helps to think in terms of a series of overlapping landscapes from the Forest of Dean or the Cotswolds, to the Mendips, to Cranborne Chase, Exmoor, Dartmoor and west into Cornwall, peopled on the one hand by its farming communities and the infrastructure supporting them, but on the other by artisans, cheesemakers among them, who have chosen to live outside towns. It's a mixture that bears no relation to the peasant cultures of France, Italy or Spain, where the values of regional or seasonal produce have been recognised and defended before they could be undermined and where the best Camembert or Roquefort is regarded as a national treasure.

A shared, almost romantic admiration for the quality of continental cheeses explains in part why many British pioneers started. Ironically, it has also turned out to be a reason why their own rarely taste like the originals that fired their imagination. For example, Sharpham, a Brie-like cheese using Jersey milk, has a colour, texture and richness not found in the more fruity Brie de Meaux from the Ile de France, which has a pedigree hundreds of years old. The raw material, the climate, the location and whoever is making the cheese all introduce variables that ensure that the gap between modern British and classic French stays healthily wide. By contrast, Lubborn's Somerset Brie is neither better nor worse than similar cheeses made in large cheeseries across the Channel because it has been conceived and executed as a me-too product.

Part of the attraction of *prodotti tipici or produits artisanaux* is that, rightly or wrongly, they seem to be linked to the ethos of the Good Life, the belief that 'small' really is 'beautiful'. It amounts, as any farmer who knows better would confirm, to a mixture of innocence and ignorance about the countryside in equal measures. What distinguishes cheesemakers, a trait they appear to share regardless of their individual motives for going into the business, is that long after any starry-eyed illusions have been lost, they still seem to be passionately attached to the miracle of turning milk into cheese. It's a trait that winemakers would recognise.

That there are cheesemakers with covert attachments to New Age thinking shouldn't come as a surprise. It is more curious that the lure of the casein has been so strong that some farmers have given up their sheep, cattle or goats to pursue the mysterious craft. The attraction, sometimes to the point of obsession, isn't easy to pin down, but it has to do with the absorbing, fascinating alchemy of turning a liquid into a solid. During the transformation so many minute factors can influence the outcome that anyone who makes a cheese cannot but feel a deep sense of achievement when he or she gets it right.

No details are insignificant to a cheesemaker, but each one singles out those he or she feels to have the most influence. One argues that cows should always be on open pasture. Another is more concerned about the ratio of protein to fat in the milk. One believes that the animal rennet used as a coagulant is better for the development of flavours; a second prefers a vegetarian one; a third will use vegetarian rennet so long as it hasn't been synthesised from a genetically modified source material. How to stir or cut the curds and in which direction and for how long are matters that will keep cheesemakers talking long into the night. They all guard the secrets of their starter cultures – the bacteria added to the milk to ripen it – as though they were magic powders.

Maturing the finished cheeses would seem to belong to the realm of the Black Arts. How high is the room in which they are kept? How often should they be turned, or wiped, or washed? What colours are the moulds on them? What kind of wood are they sitting on? How damp is it? How dry? How warm? What invisible moulds or bacteria or enzymes are at work? How long to leave them? The anticipation of watching a cheese ripen, knowing that it is only partly under the control of the maker, probably stimulates his or her brain in the same way that the revolving roulette wheel excites the gambler.

Almost any new handmade cheese launched in England, whether it's first sold in restaurants, delicatessens or at farmers' markets, arrives like an innocent. Unless it's competing for shelf-space at

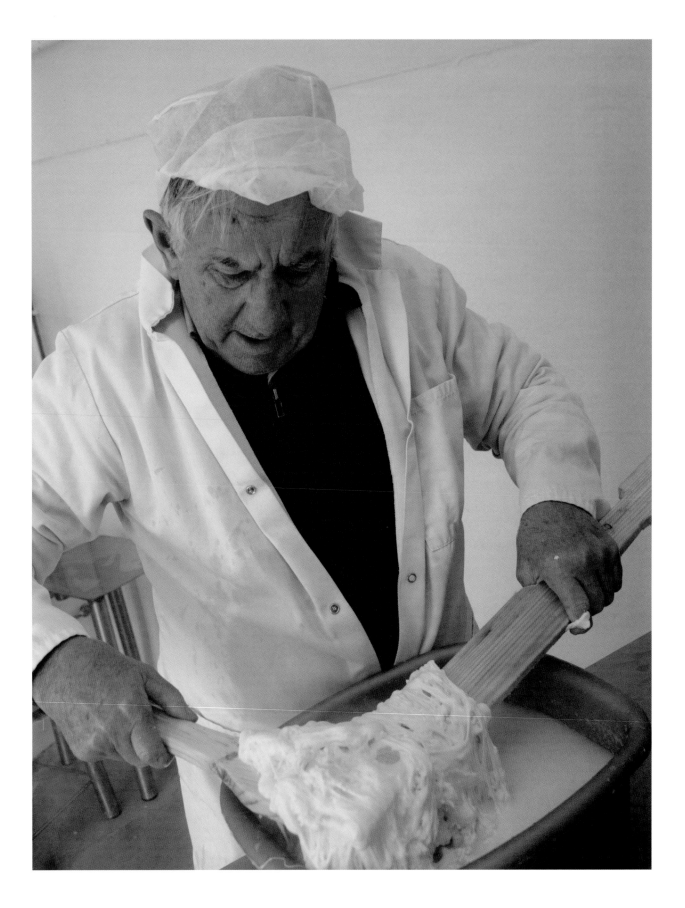

Neal's Yard Dairy, Randolph Hodgson's flagship emporium in Borough Market where customers can discriminate between what's passable, good or outstanding, it will receive a sympathetic welcome. In part this may be because it's an honorary member of the counterculture that wills any product beyond the gravitational pull of multiple retailing to be good and anything inside it to be suspect. Novelty may also have something to do with its instant acceptance. So, too, may holidays spent nosing round Le Marché Forville in Cannes or the Boqueria in Barcelona.

Survival is another matter. Some manage on the strength of their presentation or a name or clever packaging; they may even graduate to the shelves of Waitrose and Sainsbury's. Some plug into the network of farmers' markets and do well enough, or find wholesalers who can keep their business ticking over. Some get by. A few fail outright. Success or lack of it doesn't always depend on

how good to eat a cheese is.

Fashion has nudged cheesemakers hither and thence. Not much more than a generation ago, goats were considered as pets. There was no record of them being farmed for their milk in the South West, let alone valued for the cheese made from such milk. Today goats' cheese comes fresh or mature, soft or hard, steeped in oil or coated in ashes from smallholdings with no more than six goats and factories buying their milk from large herds.

Mould-ripened cheeses – think Brie – have changed from being French and exotic into a routine purchase. Blue cheese used to mean Stilton or Danish Blue. Without looking beyond the six counties of the West Country, it's possible to unearth crumbly, gooey, runny, creamy, rubbery, hard, sharp 'blues', made from goats', ewes', cows' and buffaloes' milk. Speaking of which, a Devonshire farmer makes a mean *mozzarella di buffala*.

When the Beckenham cheesemonger, James

Aldridge, started rinsing a small Caerphilly cheese made on the Somerset Levels in wine and brine to create Tornegus, only committed foodies would have known that he was changing it into a washed-rind cheese. Currently, there are some, Alderwood, for instance, made on the fringes of Cranborne Chase, that compete on quality with any continental opposition and others, say, Stinking Bishop from the Forest of Dean, that have surfed a wave of media publicity.

The new cheeses aren't equally wonderful. Ones that have started off metaphorically full of holes, have carried off the ugly duckling trick of turning into swans, but not all. It takes years of practice before most evolve to their ideal condition. Taints, tangs and tinges lurk in them. One week they are rubbery, the next they may be sliding over the counter. Translate the defects in many 'hand-crafted' cheeses to a commercial cheesery and the plant would close.

Defining how cheese should taste can be simple: it can be virtually impossible. For the classic, hard territorials, there are professional graders and buyers who have no difficulty working within an agreed framework. With the rest much relies on the untutored subjective opinion of the taster. Perhaps that is as it should be given that they rely on their distinctiveness. There's rarely a question of comparing like with like.

What is refreshing about the lack of certainty is that, although there may be individual judges competent enough to deconstruct the composition and gustatory profile of any lump of curd, the pleasures of cheese-eating haven't been circumscribed, as with wine, by an encyclopaedia of information with it's own lexicon of techno-speak. It may be appropriate to relate the aromas in a Bordeaux to raspberries, black currants, liquorice or even leather. Although a cheese may smell of peach or almonds, it loses something in the imagination by analysis of this kind.

If that sounds unconvincing, try picturing the scent of a peach in terms of a ripe Camembert. Conversely, 'freshly mown grass' or 'hay' does create a vivid image that may enhance one's enjoyment of a particular taste conveyed by some cheeses because the connection is direct and appropriate. Going hunting for the more obscure substrate of flavour compounds is an unnecessary wild goose chase that turns a delicious everyday food into a game for wannabe sophisticates.

According to the novelist G.K. Chesterton: 'Poets have been mysteriously silent on the subject of cheese.' This is no accident.

Pierre Androuët, the most renowned French cheesemonger of the twentieth century, prefaced his *Guide du Fromage*, which is flawless on French cheeses and flawed on British ones, with two letters to his daughter. In it the affection he felt for her was echoed by his love not only of the cheeses that he matured with such care in his shop near the Gare St Lazare, but also his passion for France's countryside.

The cheesemakers of the West Country are helping to give the region a new sense of purpose, a direction at a time when the traditional rules and tenets of what the country *is* are being re-written. The amazing thing about them as a body is that they have had such an impact, so soon. Who they are is the subject of this book. It traces their aspirations, their commitment, their obsessions.

At the outset of this introduction I mentioned one, for me, special cheese. In the course of researching this book, I've sampled hundreds, many of which were delicious, a few were disastrous, and some sublime. A large proportion of them are listed in the Gazetteer in Part Two, which provides details of all the cheesemakers in the West Country. In the mid-twentieth century, I would have been hard pressed to find ten.

The pioneers behind modern cheesemaking aren't revolutionaries, nor do they have flowers in their hair, but they have enriched the quality of life.

Tasting Cheese

I can't think of anything worse than that the simple pleasure of eating cheese should drape itself in the multi-coloured costume of wine tasting with its arcane vocabulary, learnt and shared by initiates but incomprehensible to the rest of us.

On the other hand, if we are going to value cheese we should take a little trouble when tasting it, if only for the first bite. If we don't, then we might as well lump all kinds together. Professional graders, so I've been told, don't taste. They simply measure a sample against objective criteria. Well, we don't belong to that fraternity either, so this is a kind of rough-and-ready guide as to how you or I might sum up quickly whether a cheese works for us.

1 First impressions count, so don't reject them out of hand.
2 Look at the cheese.
3 Touch it, break it, smell it.
4 Put a piece in your mouth, chew it, even press it against the roof of the mouth. What can you taste? How does it feel?
5 Swallow it and think: 'What's left behind?'

In a little more detail:

When you look at it, what sort of a rind does it have? The outside doesn't matter that much, but a thick, crusty rind on a hard cheese covered in a powdery dust, beyond what might be expected from natural moulds, could indicate cheese mites. Cracks in the rind may be a clue to taints.

When you smell it make up your mind about the intensity of the aroma and whether it's both what you expected and what you find appealing.

A potent-smelling cheese can also have as delicate and appetising an aroma as a gentle-smelling one. A bland cheese can be bland and nothing else. If something seems not quite right, be suspicious. Rotten or tainted is just that, not some creative cheesemaker's trick.

Texture ranges from fresh cream cheese to rock hard with every kind of imaginable variation in between. In any given style of cheese, choosing what appeals to you is the key thing. Take a French cheese such as Camembert. Go to a market and you'll find customers prodding individual ones until their experience tells them that they have found something with the degree of ripeness they enjoy. They aren't all looking for the same qualities. Some like a hard chalky thread in the middle; others want a cheese that will almost run when cut. Trust your own judgement.

When you taste at the most basic level, decide whether the cheese, if you know it already, tastes as you expect it to: for instance, is this cheddar? Next, fix in your mind where it fits on an imaginary scale between tasteless and overpowering. Is it sweet or salty? Then, you can begin to appreciate flavour details. Is the cheese buttery, pleasantly lactic, sharp, harsh, bitter? And can you pick out fresh vegetal flavours such as grass, or dried fruit or nuts. I'd stop there, but there are those who know more than me who will talk about specific spices or caramel or floral aromas.

What does matter is the last impression. Here, I guess it's very personal, but words like balanced or rounded reflect a positive sense of the overall experience. That's a sort of final arbiter. Good cheese is moreish. The first mouthful should leave your mouth crying out for more – that's why good cheesemongers who trust their own judgement want customers to try before they buy.

Part One
the cheesemakers

The Cheese's Champion

Charles Martell owns a smallholding of rare-breed cattle, pigs, ducks and chickens in a corner of the straggling Gloucestershire parish of Dymock, part of the Royal Forest of Dean – that idealised stretch of countryside between the River Wye and the Severn Estuary. A committed, active conservationist, he has brought together a national collection of the county's apple varieties. For a hobby, he trained a team of oxen to plough his land. He can also claim to have been instrumental in saving both Double and Single Gloucester from extinction as farmhouse cheeses, surviving merely in factories.

What's the difference between them? Double Gloucester rates as the senior partner. It's made from the full-cream milk of evening and morning milking. Dusty, with a mottled mould, made in the shape of a small millstone, it's ready to eat at about six months old. One of the myths about this cheese is that farmers would jump up and down on it to check that the rind didn't split before sending it to market. Cut into, it's hard, brittle almost, like chocolate with a buttery taste. It was probably the earliest English territorial to be coloured with the vegetable dye annatto that was imported from the New World by adventurers

Above: Traditional wheels of cheese from the Forest of Dean.
Opposite: Charles Martell pats two of his favourite Gloucester cows.

Above: Cattle have a white strip, the 'finchback' running down their backs and along the tail. Opposite: Cheeses had to be hard enough to stand on before they were marketed.

such as Francis Drake and Walter Raleigh in Elizabeth I's reign.

Single Gloucester was sometimes known as 'hay cheese', because it was made in winter when the cattle were kept indoors, more often from skimmed or half-skimmed milk. It was young, moist, white, and eaten on the farm before any taints had a chance of spoiling the taste. Double wasn't a winter option, because the hygiene in most barns would have been primitive, unsuitable to any long-keeping cheese intended for sale at market. Unattractive to the factory dairies of the twentieth century, Single Gloucester would have become extinct, but for Charles.

Whereas cheddar has never been linked to any particular breed of cow, the Gloucesters' past is tied to beautiful horned chestnut or black cattle with a distinctive white tail that continues as a narrow strip along the backbone, that has survived 'cattle plague', foot-and-mouth and tuberculosis as well as changing fashions in husbandry.

These cattle, called Gloucesters or Old Gloucesters, were flourishing, though not as a controlled pedigree breed, when Daniel Defoe, *Robinson Crusoe*'s author, recognised the cheese's importance during his travels about England:

'All the lower part of this county [Wiltshire], and also of Gloucestershire, adjoining, is full of large feeding farms, which we call dairies, and the cheese they make, as it is excellent good of its kind, so being a different kind from the Cheshire, being soft and thin, is eaten newer than that from Cheshire. Of this, a vast quantity is every week sent up to London, where, though it is

called Gloucestershire cheese, yet a great part of it is made in Wiltshire, and the greatest part of that which comes to London, the Gloucestershire cheese being more generally carried to Bristol and Bath, where a very great quantity is consumed, as well by the inhabitants of two populous cities, as also for the shipping off to our West-India colonies, and other places.'

The Cattle Plague of 1748 decimated stock and shut down markets, but Gloucesters survived to be recognised as a distinct breed following the creation of a herd on the Badminton estate in 1805. Thereafter, numbers expanded and contracted, but had shrunk to less than seventy when Charles Martell, a zoology graduate, purchased a bull and two cows to rear at Laurel Farm, the ten-acre smallholding he acquired in 1972. Back then 'conservation' was, according to him, a dirty word. Those who attempted to practise it were, he was told, 'Stupid – they should be doing proper farming'.

He set out to do with his two cows what Gloucesters had been famed for: cheesemaking. At the time it may have seemed a half-baked New Age gesture. It nevertheless had deep roots. When he was six his grandmother gave him *A Beast Book for the Pocket* which carried an illustration of an Old Gloucester cow and the caption: 'This old breed was saved from extinction thanks to the introduction of a livestock register in 1919. In 1935 there were 130 registered head of cattle. Its milk was particularly suited for making cheese.'

If the inspiration was quixotic, he had chosen an appropriate spot. Since Norman days, the head of the Dymock family (Charles' mother was a Dymock), from which the village takes its name, holds the symbolic title of Royal Champion at the coronation of a British monarch. His role is to throw down the gauntlet and ask whether anyone challenges the heir apparent's right to the throne.

Should anyone come forward he must fight him on the king or queen's behalf.

Charles' aspiration was checked at a basic level by never having made any cheese, let alone Single or Double. This difficulty was compounded by the fact that as a craft skill, there was almost nobody left to teach him. He was helped, though, by a Miss Colner, the then Ministry of Agriculture's regional Dairy Husbandry Advisor, who gave him her own recipes and watched him make his first Single Gloucester.

Above: Martell's dairy on his smallholding at Dymock is run on strict conservationist lines.
Opposite: Blossom from the Stinking Bishop pear that lent its name to a cheese.

Her advice put him to work, but it didn't turn him into an expert overnight. It certainly didn't pay for his keep and he drove trucks to make ends meet.

Because he was treating his milk much as a dairymaid a century earlier might have, he had to

St Briavel's Bread and Cheese Dole

BRIAVELS (St.), a village, a parish, and a hundred, in Gloucester. The village stands near Offa's Dyke and the river Wye, 4½ miles SSW of Coleford, and 5 NW of Woolaston r. station; and has a post office under Coleford. It formerly was a market-town; and it long made a figure as a defence-post against the Welsh.

Imperial Gazetteer of England and Wales (1870–2)

On Whit Sunday, outside St Mary's Church a medieval pageant takes place at which a basket of bread and cheese is thrown out – 'doled out' – to the gathered throng of villagers, who catch it in hats, skirts or by any other means they can.

According to oral tradition the custom goes back to the Middle Ages, but the first written account is a mere 230 years old. Anyone who captured a piece of the dole could exchange it, together with a penny, for the right to gather wood from the neighbouring woods during the following year. By the nineteenth century, the dole had turned into a bun fight when, according to a contemporary magazine, 'most of the food was used as pellets; the pastor coming in for his share as he left the pulpit'.

At the time, the chief local industry was mining and miners used to keep pieces of the 'dole' in matchboxes as a superstitious charm against accidents.

Farmhouse Gloucester cheese became extinct before Martell revived it.

experience the same seasonal fluctuations, the same inconsistencies, the same thrill when a batch turned out well, the same disappointment when it didn't. He learned the hard way how slamming a door or leaving a window ajar, buying a new piece of equipment, or introducing a fresh pair of hands into the dairy, can play havoc. More than once he buried a batch of cheeses in a hole in the ground, leaving it to rot.

Agricultural or food historians often find it impossible to reconstruct what cheeses were like in the distant past. Martell's cheeses, made from raw milk, would have been familiar on any Victorian board. A record from the mid-Georgian period in William Marshall's, *The Rural Economy of Glocestershire* (1783) shows that the method has remained constant for much longer, that two very similar varieties were produced on farms.

The most curious difference though is that the names for the two kinds seem to have been inverted. 'One meal cheese', possibly the source of the epithet 'Single', or 'Best Making' was produced from full-cream milk. In theory, 'Two meal cheese' was, supposedly, a mixture of the previous evening's milking skimmed and added to the morning's milking, except that the dairy 'superintendent' often economised by skimming her morning milk too.

If that's not confusing enough, there's another historical twist. After being pressed, salted and scraped, the immature cheeselings were taken to a ripening chamber to be laid on a floor that had been blackened by rubbing it with bean-tops or potato stalks, because it helped the formation of

Aligot of Mayhill Green

David Everitt-Matthias of the Champignon Sauvage, Cheltenham, uses Charles Martell's Mayhill Green for his own individual take on an Auvergnat speciality. The cheese has a springy texture and is flavoured by nettles. An effective alternative would be to replace it with Stinking Bishop and add a tablespoon of chopped nettles or herbs. Accompany with young, seasonal vegetables … and Gloucester Old Spot sausages. The Champignon Sauvage, a Michelin 2-star restaurant dishes it up with partridge.

Serves 4–6

60g rendered bacon fat (not smoked)
800g peeled, waxy potatoes
250g Mayhill Green cheese
100ml crème fraîche (optional)
freshly ground black pepper
possibly a little salt

Warm the fat in a steep-sided saucepan that will take the potatoes with plenty of room to spare. Slice the potatoes thinly. Add them to the pan and coat them in the fat. Lower the heat, cover and cook until the potatoes are done. Make sure they don't start to colour. You can add a tablespoon of water every time you check them. It will take 15–20 minutes.

Chop up the cheese. When the potatoes are tender and starting to break up, beat them well with a wooden spoon until they are like mash. Incorporate the cheese, keeping the pan over the heat. Continue to beat and lift the mixture. When the cheese has melted into the potato, take the pan off the heat and beat the 'aligot' some more. If you want to add the crème fraîche, do it now. Stir in pepper. Add a little salt according to taste – it's a matter of personal taste – and serve, piping hot.

The Randwick Wap

Randwick is a small but populous village eight miles south of Gloucester, and two miles from the market town of Stroud … The summit of the hill, on the slope of which the village stands called 'Randwick Ash' commands a beautiful and extensive view of the River Severn, Wales, and the surrounding counties; and the ash tree, which gives its name to the spot, forms a landmark for miles.'

A History of Randwick by E. P. Fennemore (1892)

The current Randwick Wap, held the second Sunday in May, is a revival of a centuries' old tradition. It starts with a procession led by the Mop Man, followed by a High Sheriff, cheese-bearers and the appointed mayor, accompanied by his consort, and ends by the village pond. Here, the mayor is ceremoniously soused in the water, before the Mop Man runs about spraying, splashing and daubing anyone within reach with his mop. The party ends with a cheese-rolling race down the steep slope of Well Leaze.

In the eighteenth and nineteenth centuries it was a general holiday for the surrounding villages. The festivities lasted from the Saturday night with the mayor's election for up to a week and was characterised by drunkenness, feasting and sport. Villagers stuck a bough outside their homes to advertise the fact they had cider to sell. Gypsies told fortunes and hawkers pedalled mutton pies. Complaints about pagan debauchery had no effect upon the Randwick Wap, which was protected by ancient law until it suddenly ended in 1893.

desirable blue mould — echoed today by the nettles of Cornish Yarg (see Nettle Cheese section). Once the floor was covered by a single layer of cheeses, the oldest ones were 'doubled' or stacked 'three or four double'.

The region also enjoyed a reputation for a now vanished Sage Cheese, made the same way as Single, but coloured with sage, parsley and marigold leaves, that must have been similar to the Sage Derby still being made in the Midlands.

Charles Martell may not scrub the floor with assorted vegetation, nor does he milk his cows under an apple tree in the 'cowground'. He doesn't labour from 4 a.m. until bedtime as dairymaids on the larger farms did. He can empathise with the importance placed on hygiene by William Marshall back in 1783: 'With respect to CLEANLINESS, the Glocesterhire dairywomen stand unimpeachable. Judging from the dairies I have seen, they are much above par *in reality* — though not so to common appearance.'

Back then, the factors (wholesalers) who bought Gloucesters paid a premium for the cream-rich 'Best Making', but the difference was a few shillings per hundredweight. Martell relates to this because he feels that the quality of his Single matches the Double because his herd grazes on old pastures, rich in white clover. He has identified more than 100 plants growing in his meadows and since coming to Dymock has only seen one, Meadow Saffron, disappear. The reason why Double costs more than Single is less to do with ingredients or quality than the time spent ageing it, six months as opposed to six weeks.

Having taught himself the intricacies of a dairymaid's skills, he still had to sell what he was grafting so hard to make. For over ten years, he had a cheese stall at Cirencester Market, where he sold factory Double Gloucester — 'Really quite good' – alongside his own. Being at the sharp end gave him insights into the gulf that exists between those customers brought up on mild and processed brands and the small minority that sought variety in texture and degrees of intensity in taste.

Eventually he sold the stall to buy more land. By then, he was already able to earn a living from his own cheeses, doubtless assisted by an unexpected flush of media attention. 'We were at a show with my eighteen-month daughter and she won the prize for the best ridden donkey. The local Press asked: "You've got a donkey; what else do you have?" I said, "We've got Gloucester cows and make Double Gloucester cheese." By the end of the week three national dailies had picked up the story.'

By increasing his holding, Charles was able to focus more closely on conservation. Already he was buying Gloucester Old Spot pigs, who were fed on the whey that is a by-product of cheesemaking. He was training oxen to till the soil for the fields that produced his cattle feed. They were a casualty of tuberculosis, but handling them, conscious of their strength, left him with the conviction that man's success as a primate is founded on his ability to yoke other species to his will. The ox is many times stronger than the ploughman guiding him, yet it obeys.

He indulged his hobby of collecting old varieties of the county's apples, documenting their history and planting trees in his orchard, to the point where he now holds the national collection. It includes Leathercoat, mentioned by Shakespeare, Jenny Lind (named after a famous actress), Lemon Pippin of Gloucestershire and Kill-Boys, a cider apple reputed for its lethal effect. Similarly he helped create a parallel collection of perry pears that is kept at the Three Counties Showground in Malvern. His interest here led him to come across a variety called Stinking Bishop, which he used for another cheese he makes at Laurel Farm.

At Laurel Farm he practises a kind of conservation-led farming that respects both land and livestock. His methods have won him a prestigious international prize, the 'Premio Slow Food' for the Defense of Biodiversity, that has previously been awarded to a village co-operative in Bukina Fasso, an Ethiopian seed bank and a Mexican Director of Popular Culture with a special interest in the history of Mexican food.

By developing a niche for the cheese, he has gone a long way to ensure the future of the breed that was his principle aim. How many others have followed his lead? Still too few. There may be three or four dairies with Gloucester cows that are milked for their cheese, but the breed is recovering. From the handful that were left when he bought the farm, there are now several hundred, scattered, it is true, around the country, but no longer endangered. If the other side of the coin is that Martell has gained the experience to become a highly regarded specialist cheesemaker, he should be doubly satisfied.

Stinking Bishop

Stinking Bishop isn't an insult directed at a local ecclesiast past or present, but it is the nickname of an unsavoury Gloucestershire character, an eponymous

Blossom, Jenner and the first inoculation

Sir Edward Jenner took his first anti-smallpox serum from Blossom, a Gloucester cow, in 1796, hence the word 'vaccination' from the Latin *vacca* – a cow. Her hide was later donated to St George's Hospital in London by Jenner's family, where it is still kept at the Medical School Library.

farmer with a reputation for a fiery temper who on one occasion shot his kettle because the water in it wouldn't boil. Living in mid-Victorian days, he was credited with growing, either by chance or design, a pear whose juice made admirable perry. Since the variety is also known by at least three other names – Moorcroft, Choke and Malvern Hills – all equally venerable, nobody knows its true roots.

Charles Martell borrowed the name for a cheese that he has invented, no question. The name does point obliquely towards the smell, that is like over-ripe fruit and akin to the decomposition sometimes smelled in hedges or by the roadside. It weighs about three pounds, is a flat disc with a sticky burnt-orange rind. Cut open, it may just hold its shape or bulge slightly, or when very ripe it almost spreads outwards. The taste is much milder than one might expect, almost sweet. Its parent is right when he

says, 'The bark is worse than the bite.'

He likes to think of it as a monastery cheese, one that might have been produced by monks pre-Reformation, but there isn't any evidence. Instead, he can point to French washed-rind cheeses such as Burgundian Epoisses or Norman Pont L'Evêque, which do have strong ties to Cistercian abbeys.

It's a cheese that took years of gestation and tinkering before reaching its present form, but it owes its existence to Martell's passion for the region's apples and pears. While he was still working Cirencester Market in the 1980s, he came across a new Irish cheese called Milleens that he liked and wondered whether he could develop something comparable. At the same period, he discussed the technicalities with his friend, the legendary cheesemonger James Aldridge, who was taking miniature Caerphillies and washing them in wine. The two men collaborated. For

These pages: Stinking Bishop is a powerful-smelling washed-rind cheese that became instantly famous when it was used in a Wallace and Gromit film.

a while Martell sent fresh cheese for Aldridge to wash the curd and ripen it. When that didn't achieve the desired results he experimented at home until he had a reliable recipe. That was in 1994.

Since then, it has had several makeovers before winning Best New Cheese at the British Cheese Awards ten years on.

At the outset, he had thought of it as another opportunity to use the milk from his Gloucester herd. Since then, the demand for Single and Double has been such that he can't afford to set any aside for Stinking Bishop. Instead, he buys in 300-gallon batches of Friesian milk that goes to a separate dairy on his smallholding where his Russian wife

Natasha is the dairymaid in charge of making it every day. What hasn't altered is the reliance on perry to wash the young curds. He takes the pears from his own trees to a local perry-maker who presses and ferments them for him.

Rolling out 100 cheeses a day could be considered an achievement by the standards of many of his peers. Martell's gentle cottage industry routine was shocked by the launch of a hit Wallace and Gromit animation movie *The Curse of the Were-Rabbit*, which features Stinking Bishop. Even before the film's premiere word had gone about and his order book had run out of space. He isn't driven, though, by ambition for material success. Whatever he can produce without disturbing his way of life at Laurel Farm, he will, but he isn't about to convert his farm to a factory or move production to an industrial estate.

Pineapples and Pyramids

Cerney House, between Cirencester and Cheltenham, manages to look substantial without being ostentatious, not so much the property of old money, but rather one for a modern captain of industry, such as Sir Michael Angus, who has overseen businesses as diverse as Boots, Unilever and Whitbread.

Since buying the family home, three personal passions have flourished: his wine cellar (not open to the public), a showpiece Victorian garden (that is), and goats' cheese, begun as a hobby by his wife Lady Isabel and now a thriving enterprise. Lady Isabel and her daughter Barbara oversee the business that produces 500, seven-ounce, oak-ash-powdered Cerneys each week at a dinky dairy, tucked away in the pretty Cotswold

village of North Cerney.

According to Barbara, goats were already part of Lady Isabel's life when they moved to Gloucestershire from Hertfordshire: 'It was like Noah's Ark. We had goats, chickens, lorries arriving filled with animals. Goodness knows what people thought when they first saw us.'

Having settled in, Lady Isabel set up headquarters in the pantry and began teaching herself how to turn milk into cheese. Her enthusiasm as well as her ambitions were coloured by having lived for several

Above: Cerney is a picture-postcard Cotswold village near the market town of Cirencester. Opposite: Cheesemaker, Barbara Johnson (née Angus) with husband Angus.

These pages: Soft, fresh, pyramid-shaped curds of Cerney cheese are dusted with a fine black-ash coating before being packed.

years in Paris where *fromage de chèvre* was as commonplace as it was rare in England. She could have picked picodon, pelardon, crottin, chèvreton, chabichou or St Maure or any of a dozen other varieties, but she set out to imitate the truncated pyramid shape, if not the aging, of Valençay, a speciality of Touraine and coincidentally, the same cheese that Mary Holbrook, outside Bath, had chosen as her model for Tymsboro (see p.50).

With Barbara helping, she progressed to a level where she could consider selling her surplus. Her maiden customer was an ex-England cricketer, Charlie Barnett, who ran a fish shop in Cirencester after his retirement. Enthusiastic she may have been, determined too, but few millionaires' wives want to roll up their sleeves and work full-time in a dairy. Her primary interest (and her daughter's) lay in reviving a neglected garden without the aid of twenty-four gardeners who had once maintained it. Her difficulty was that she had committed five years to developing Cerney cheese. She was

attached to it, didn't want to give it up.

Enter Marion Conisbee-Smith, accompanied by a herd of Golden Guernseys, a rare breed with French, Syrian and Maltese ancestry. She had been hoping to export the milk, but the deal had fallen through. Lady Isabel agreed to bail her out; it would help to increase her cheesemaking capacity. She was also astute enough to offer the goats' owner the job of milkmaid and cheesemaker.

She had picked well. Marion had just returned to the Cotswolds after her marriage had broken up. She was at a loose end. She also had a National Diploma in Dairying, had made Cheddar in Devon and worked in the laboratories of Express Dairies. Accepting, she recalled, wasn't a planned career move: 'I hummed and haaed and then I thought "I'm never going to make a fortune"; if you're doing something you really enjoy and can still survive, why not?'

Once her employer realised that Marion could take control she was only too willing to stand back: 'She was far more interested in the garden and wanted to be outside, happy to let someone go on with things so long as she was satisfied with what went on.'

It was a relationship that lasted sixteen years during which elite cheesemongers such as Arthur

Cunynghame of Paxton & Whitfield and Baron Puget of the Oxford Cheese Company, helped to spread Cerney's reputation. From the pantry in the big house, Marion moved the dairy to Chapel Farm, in North Cerney. Designed like a laboratory, impeccably clean, it was laid out to pre-empt any risks that might arise from using raw milk. She lived 'above the shop', on hand, watchful, sensitive to any hint of a problem.

Essentially, a fresh cheese should be one of the simplest to produce. After the starter and rennet have been added, it's left twenty-four to thirty-six hours for the curd to form, after which it is part-drained and then ladled into moulds and, when firm, coated with a blend of ash and salt. Nursing the milk through its transformation is the hard part.

The goats transmit a residual taste of what they eat to the milk, as do other ruminants, only more so. Hot, close, muggy weather can also alter the milk's character.

It can't be forced to follow a schedule. Marion had to react to whatever tricks a batch might be playing on her. 'It did rule my life. If it was going to be slow one day, you'd have to go with it. If it didn't break within a couple of hours, you'd have

Cooper's Hill Cheese Rolling

BROCKWORTH, a parish in the district and county of Gloucester; on Ermine-street, in the vale of Gloucester … Cooper's Hill, a steep projection from neighbouring hills, commands a brilliant view.
Imperial Gazetteer of England and Wales (1870–2)

The annual cheese rolling at Cooper's Hill used to be held on midsummer eve, but has moved to the Whitsun Bank Holiday. Without question it's the most dangerous folk custom still permitted in the British Isles. For most participants it's a virility test, which probably justifies the claim that it was instituted centuries back as a fertility rite.

Run as a race, it's a mad 200-metre dash after a wood-encased nine-pound Double Gloucester, down a gradient that varies between 1:2 and 1:1.

Before the start. the waiting crowd of several thousands roar: 'Roll that cheese!' The runners sit at the starting line waiting for the off, then launch themselves down a slope of grass tufts, decomposing leaf litter, slick grass, tussocks, holes in the ground and a few stray snails. The cheese reaches a speed of 120 kph. Nobody catches it, though the race winner gets to keep it. There are no recent records of fatalities, although in 1998 there were eighteen injuries among competitors, mostly broken bones or cuts, and several more among spectators, hit either by runaway cheeses or somersaulting racers.

The epitaph of one legendary bystander reads:

Here lies Billy, if you please
Hit in the stomach with a cheese
Cheese is wholesome fayre, they say
It turned poor Billy into clay.

Cerney House is as renowned for its manicured gardens as it is for its cheese.

to go back to it and that's what I did.'

'Break' in her parlance refers to a critical moment in the setting of a tight curd. It describes what happens when a finger prods the coagulated milk. If it's ready, it breaks cleanly and whey runs into the gap. Any of half a dozen reasons might prevent it doing so, of which the most likely would be the presence of uninvited bacteria, but it might also be down to heat, cold, the milk's freshness, the rennet or human error.

Marion toyed and tinkered with dosing and blending starters. What is it about this arcane practice that so excites cheesemakers almost without exception? These bacteria cultures have the role of developing lactic acid in the milk and there are literally dozens on the market. How they are used and which ones and in what combination is perhaps the only part in the whole process where the maker exerts some control. It's a bit like adding basil to a stew, rather than thyme, or basil mixed with thyme, or basil, thyme and oregano, where quantities, balance and timing influence the end result, and add a kind of signature. In cheesemaking, however, starters affect texture and moisture content as well as flavour. In a fresh cheese especially, where maturation doesn't enter the equation, they define the taste.

That Cerney evolved and for the better is due to Marion's dedication, but it wasn't the only factor. Her geriatric goats and those belonging to Lady Isabel eventually died. Rather than replace them, they switched to buying milk from an outside commercial herd, something that would have been inconceivable back in the pantry days, because then there were no suppliers.

It may not square with romantics, who relate to the idea of goats wandering over the landscape nibbling every piece of vegetation they find, but because they eat practically the same feed every day, it does improve the regularity of the milk. It never bothered Marion that the herds were kept indoors: 'They are quite lazy animals that like their bed and breakfast.'

Just how good at her job she had become was confirmed when Cerney was chosen as the Supreme Champion from over 700 entries at the British Cheese Awards in 2000. The dairy also struck Gold four years later for Cerney Pepper, a smaller fresh goats' cheese coated in cracked peppercorns.

Unfortunately Marion's long-standing relationship with Lady Isabel was about to turn sour. Marion was diagnosed as suffering from multiple sclerosis. Her absences from the dairy were frequent enough to impact upon its smooth running and she was asked to leave. 'We didn't part on the best of terms,' Marion recalled. Losing her job also meant that she lost the roof over her head. She discovered the hard way that there is little room for sentiment in any business, even a micro one.

For Marion it hurt a lot. A 'terrible year' followed, compounded by the fact that she owned eight Gloucester cows and had nowhere to graze them. She sorted out their domestic arrangements through a 'dating agency' run by the Cotswolds Area Of Outstanding Natural Beauty that can place livestock on selected grasslands. Her own problems were solved by moving in with her partner. As a stopgap and to keep her hand in, she made Gloucester cheeses at Wick Court, a member of the Farms For City Children scheme that brings inner city kids into the countryside. In her leisure time she pursued her hobby of photographing Gloucester dovecotes.

Her major project, though, was putting together the finance to open a dairy of her own where she might, with the milk from her own cattle, re-invent a lost cheese: the Pineapple. It dates from the late-eighteenth century when the fruit was fashionable and much copied in stone as a country-garden ornament. It survived into Queen Victoria's reign; then vanished.

Its form is unique. Marion had to commission a wood turner in Birdlip to make moulds that copy the characteristic shape. The maturing is also quite unlike that of any other British cheese in that it has to be hung in a net. Weighing about three kilograms, ripened for four months, it's her take on a Double Gloucester recipe, which is more than an educated guess, because Double Gloucester has always been coloured with annatto that can give a similar tint to the fruit's flesh. She exhibited one of her first batch of unpasteurised Pineapples at the 2005 Cheese Awards, winning Bronze, a sign, she felt, that she was on the right track.

By that time she had also come up with a fresh cheese of her own with extra cream added back into the milk that's wrapped in raspberry leaves. She baptised it Finchback, after the white strips along the backs of her cows. Without financial backing, she had been relying on grants to have her dairy up and running. Caught up in bureaucratic red tape, she found it offered, withdrawn, and then offered again. In the meantime a Channel 4 camera crew filming a documentary about business start-ups was following every twist.

Her departure had an obvious impact at Cerney House. Lady Isabel did not want to close down the cheesemaking; nor would she have been able to do the labour-intensive work herself. Daughter Barbara stepped in, although it meant juggling the dairy duties with her first love, the garden, where she was already fully employed.

In their own way, the grounds have attracted as much praise as the cheese. At their heart is a gently

sloping walled garden, exuberant in summer, filled with organic fruit and vegetables, which is very personal in its layout and not, according to *The Good Gardens Guide*, for 'people who like things tickety-boo'. It produces jams, jellies, chutneys, flavoured oils and vinegars. Barbara was once a teacher and her control over her plants shares something in common with the care she might have exerted over her human charges: allow them the latitude to express themselves naturally, but keep them in check. Her top tip for gardeners is: 'Be the boss. It's important not to be intimidated by plants. I just bung them in the ground and if, after a while, one offends me, I dig it out.'

That pragmatic approach might not wash when

Above: The cheeses look as though they've been touched with sooty fingers – and they have. Opposite: 'Cheese cloths' are an essential part of the fresh cheesemaker's armoury.

making cheese. She has, though, shown the resilience to sustain the dairy, and kept it operating smoothly when it might so easily have been discarded as a toy that had ceased to amuse.

Having coped with the roller-coaster ride of fortune, Marion bears no grudges towards her former employers: 'They have done me a great favour, because I shall have my own cheese. It will be mine – whatever I do – and I can do it in my own way.'

Cotswolds Model Dairy

It's logical that the Cotswolds should trade on their quaintness. Every village seems freshly swept, so tidy that it might be a film set and probably has been. Sandstone buildings cluster together in harmonious groups, usually around a fifteenth-century church. In this cosseted region, five miles outside Stow-on-the-Wold, Lady Carole Bamford has turned a simple dairy farm into an exquisite piece of holistic retail theatre, centred around food produced on the estate: fruit, vegetables, meat, bread, butter and cheese. As Daylesford Organic Farm has flourished, she has added clothes, beauty therapy and garden ornamentation. And it all started with a cheese, not any ordinary one, but the eponymous

Daylesford that, still a virtual newcomer, has been hailed as 'The best cheese in England'.

When Lady Carole made up her mind to transform the farm into an organic temple, her first step was to turn the cows' milking parlour into a dairy. Light, spacious, equipped with the best hardwood-clad Dutch vats and Gouda presses, it gives the impression of purposefulness, but also a concern for those working there that contrasts strongly with those functional cheese factories that smell of regurgitated milk and the cubby-holes of the smallest makers working on a shoestring.

The dairy's design, layout and mood is down to the American cheesemaker she hired. Joe Schneider had been living in Holland, making

Greek feta for a Turkish employer. Having crossed the North Sea, and after a spell learning about ripening hard cheeses in Sussex, he moved to Daylesford with a virtual free hand to make things happen: 'I was the first one here. There was no farm shop; that was a grain barn. Nothing existed in its current branded form. All they knew was they wanted a product. They were going to do this development and they wanted to have their own cheese.'

A qualified agricultural engineer, passionate about his craft, his plans for the dairy were a kind of nest-building exercise, devising the ideal space in which to give birth to the cheese his imagination had conceived.

A scientist himself, he felt he understood the mechanics of making cheese, the times, the temperatures, the cutting, the stirring, the pitching, the pressing – the rigorous step-by-step method that separates the liquid phase from the solids in the milk. It's comparable to the way a chef works in a kitchen. Done flawlessly, there's a certain elegance in the way the task progresses: 'It feels like it's clicking into place.'

What excited him more was the uncertainties of the craft side: 'Imagine cooking something, leaving it for a year and thinking I put too much basil in. The dairy is my kitchen, but when I get to ripen the cheese, the signs are much more subtle. How is it developing? Why is this one different from the others? And that's the part I love trying to decipher.'

Like many of his peers the dusky cylinders gestating on his shelves will play mind games on him. He wonders whether it was the milk on a certain day that behaved oddly. Was he in a bad mood on that particular morning? Or a good mood? Or does he make good cheese when he's feeling up, bad when he's down?

Opposite: The Daylesford deli counter displays produce from the farm and dairy.
Below: Exterior courtyard: not a leaf or a tile out of place.

The alchemy begins once the cheeses are stacked in rows to mature. The temperature and humidity can be controlled. Decisions about brushing, scrubbing, scraping and turning are related to the unseen, hidden life going on both inside and on the surface. Just as a potter may look for the way in which a particular glaze toasts in the kiln, Joe watches for a bluish-grey bloom developing on the bandaged rind.

Like any hard cheesemaker he must wait three or five months before ironing, to check what has been going on under the skin. Then he'll have his first taste of how the cheese is shaping up and be able to hazard an educated guess as to what it may eventually be like.

The delay between making and selling his first batch was the most stressful eight months Joe had experienced because he had no guarantee that his craftsmanship would lead to something worth eating, let alone a cheese that anyone would want to buy: 'You have that grace period, but you don't know for five months whether you're on the right track. When you iron the cheese for the first time, you're praying to the cheese gods.'

Randolph Hodgson of Neal's Yard Dairy wrote him a personal letter offering to buy, providing that the quality matched what he had been doing before moving to the Cotswolds. In the event he need not have worried because his first and every subsequent 'vintage' has sold out.

What it did for Lady Carole's grand scheme was provide a flagship product, anchored in the farm, around which she could set other outstanding organic foods. There is now a creamery next to the dairy that makes creams, yoghurts, feta, lemon curd and cultured butter, and a bakery with some of the finest sourdough loaves anywhere, and a butcher's (meat and poultry from a sister estate at Wooton in Staffordshire), and wine from a Bamford vineyard in Provence, and a market garden that grows heritage varieties of tomatoes, and a kitchen garden growing esoteric herbs …

Maturing Daylesford means playing a waiting game, very much as he painted it. Trusting the herdsman to do his job, he isn't as preoccupied with the milk as, say James Montgomery (see p.68). It comes from a pedigree Friesian herd. It's organic and unpasteurised, pumped directly to his dairy along a short pipe connecting to the milking parlour. Levels of fat or protein? He takes note, but initially it's a detail. Only in spring, when the cattle leave the barns and go out on grass, can the milk wreak havoc with his careful technology.

The 'cooking' stage, which ends with the fresh curd being packed in hoops and pressed, is almost as carefully regulated as the assembly of a Big Mac. For any of the four dairymaids who work alongside him, the routine steps that begin with starter bacteria and end with a virgin cheese, pasted with lard, rendered from the farm's own beef, and swaddled in muslin are as simple as making a paper chain. Knowing how small the pieces of curd should be after cutting or how long stirred is second nature to them. Filling the moulds is an automatic gesture for them. Setting the presses is standard.

and a café-restaurant. If that reads like advertorial, well it's very hard not to be swept away by the intelligence with which the various edible components gel.

As to the cheese: it is a cheddar, even though it's made with Dutch tools and until recently by a dedicated American, despite the fact that the curd isn't cut, stacked in blocks and milled quite like Montgomery's would do it, and regardless of the size which, at about ten kilograms, is a third of what some farmhouse cheeses weigh. It reaches its peak a little quicker too, around or before nine months. Every batch has its own quirks, but it eats differently from the classic Somerset ones, a shade moister, a touch softer, a little less acid, yet full of a flavour that's persistent, satisfying, moreish. To anyone looking for a cheese to put in a sarnie with a dollop of Branston, this is so not the one.

Nor is Penyston, the Dairy's other cheese. Only made once a week in a smaller vat, mainly for the

Opposite: 'On your bike?'
This page: Dutch presses (above) and a wood-clad Dutch vat (below) reflect Joe Schneider's experience making cheese in Holland.

shop, it's a washed-rind cheese, made as a flattish brick, or occasionally heart-shaped. Neither pungent, nor smelly, its character changes depending on whether it's eaten quite fresh at about a fortnight when it's still quite compact or at a month when it's smoother, though not runny like some.

In an interview she gave to *The Independent* on life-changing food experiences, Lady Carole chose a Mediterranean moment: 'I was at the most amazing market in Catania, Sicily. I was handed a slice of glorious Sicilian lemon with a scattering of coarse sea salt. I savoured the delights of skin, pith and fruit on the street corner of the Duomo – something so simple and yet so memorable.'

The attractive simplicity she admired, may seem divorced from the studied sophistication of the atypical farm-shopping experience that she has so conscientiously composed. The gulf really isn't so wide. She, or those she employs, has invested as much effort in sourcing let's say an organic carrot as the *contadino Siciliano* has his lemon.

Her rustic consumer emporium belongs to the Cotswold way of life where those with the means will go out of their way to seek out the best. For

them, it epitomises an aspiration, albeit patrician, to make the countryside a green and pleasant land. By no stretch of the imagination could Daylesford be charged with supplying peasant food. It aims to serve produce adapted to the British countryside and grown as well as possible.

Early in 2006 Joe Schneider quit Daylesford. He was tempted through his long association with Neal's Yard Dairy into setting up a dairy in Nottingham where he would make the first unpasteurised Stilton from a single-farm herd in generations. Currently the five remaining makers heat-treat milk that is delivered either from a co-operative of farmers or from Dairy Crest.

What he left for his successor was more than an opportunity to make 'The best cheese in England.' He wasn't taking the recipe with him; he didn't keep back some secret trick or manipulation. On the contrary, he wanted to share what he had picked up over the five years he had been there, just as other cheesemakers had shared their knowledge with him when he arrived in the UK as a rookie. Then, he recalls with fondness sharing a bottle of whisky with the chain-smoking cheesemonger James Aldridge, who collaborated with many of the pioneers. He

Opposite, left and right: The curds are cut and stirred until the pieces are smaller than peas. Right: The cheese is cut and stacked in blocks like cheddar.

gave him advice, introductions to dairies, visited him at the farm where he worked, never minced his words, even cut open the first large cheese Joe made at his wedding.

What still amazes the American is the openness that exists among his peers, the willingness to discuss freely every aspect of their work regardless of the commercial wisdom of doing so. It's a reminder that the atmosphere surrounding farmhouse cheese is rarefied. Those who succeed are no more than a blink away from those who fail.

Lady Carole's patronage has much in common with past nobility, which has supported music or the arts. Instead she has picked food. In its own way, it too deserves to be considered an art form and a talented cheesemaker has every right to think of himself as an artist.

Juliet's Glittering Prizes

Juliet Harbutt lives about two miles down the road from Daylesford Farm, just across the Oxford border in the village of Churchill. Her Cotswold stone home is in a lane running from a strange menhir-like monument to the father of Geology, William Smith. It's a sideways reminder of her own past: she qualified as a geologist in her native New Zealand. The inside of her fridge, however, tells the story of where her true passion lies. It contains a wedge of Daylesford, another of Montgomery's cheddar, a third of Beenleigh Blue, a Sardinian pecorino, and that's just four she has brought out to taste.

The founder, organiser and ringmaster of the annual British Cheese Awards, she has introduced the general public to the temptations of 'rind-washed', 'mould-ripened', 'semi-soft' and 'hard' with the zeal of a dedicated Madam showing off her new girls. She's strict, forthright, forceful, passionate and, during the awards themselves, driving on high-octane adrenaline.

Before Juliet, there have been cheese competitions, the most famous being at Nantwich in Cheshire and at the Bath & West Show. These have been insider events, run by the trade, according to the ironed and pressed grading system that assesses objectively whether there are any faults in the manufacture. A single cheese may enter several categories, for example a Stilton might compete as a whole, a display, a half, a mature and as a retail cheese.

What Juliet did was tear up the rulebook and start afresh. Instead of dispassionate, regulated judging, she introduced the subjective component of taste. Wines are measured on how they are made, and also on their aroma or flavour. That's what distinguishes one from another. Otherwise Chateau Plonk might rate as heavily as Chateau Palmer. Cheese, she reasoned, was the same. Having founded a London cheese and wine shop (Jeroboams where, although she is no longer involved – it's become a chain), she had always treated the two as closely related. Enjoyment and taste mattered to her

customers. Any judgement that disregarded these fell short of giving the full story.

'I found it so frustrating,' she recalled 'that graders graded without tasting. Think of a banana; it's a wonderful fruit but the skin is crap. You have to ask yourself how much does it matter if the rind on, say a Camembert matters if the inside is great.'

The Naval & Military Club, popularly known as the In & Out, hosted the original Cheese Awards in 1991. Instead of relying on recognised 'experts', in every category she invited a guest judge from the food media with a good palate and no specialised experience to team up with a professional grader, maker or cheesemonger. Their complementary skills shifted the balance. Cheeses had to have character, had to please the palate to earn a top prize.

Since then, the event has grown from a couple of hundred entries to around 850, with two thirds of the makers in the British Isles competing. It differs from the venerable competitions in that any cheese can only be entered in one category. No

longer, a minor initiative held in an exclusive gentleman's club, it's turned into a festival, an orgy of cheese tasting, where the public has a chance of sampling the good, bad and ugly, held in salubrious surroundings such as Blenheim Palace, with judges invited from as far afield as Japan, and camera crews and the national press hungry for a cheesy story.

It's made her friends and lost her others. Instead of focusing on small or independent makers, she has preferred to practise an inclusive approach. This isn't an exclusive shop window reserved for the specialists. There are classes where the giant block cheddar makers can and do enter, where they can win Gold Medals. At times, the judging can seem like a cattle market, when for instance, a particularly opinionated member of the press disagrees with a professional grader. Ultimately the buck stops with her. She arbitrates in disputes, decides borderline awards, and appoints the judges for the fifty-odd categories. If someone enters the wrong category,

These pages: At Daylesford, Joe Schneider preferred to 'block' the cheese on a table rather than in the vat.

she takes a unilateral decision to reroute it.

Her influences at both ends of the chain – the consumer who buys most of his or her cheese from multiple retailers and the dairy fraternity – is almost frightening, although it is generally benevolent. When she isn't setting up the awards (she does it virtually single handed), she's giving courses on tasting, consulting or giving free advice to the heterogeneous, often quirky, often isolated members of the cheese industry. She's amazed how blinkered many of the little businesses can be. 'Most cheesemakers have no idea what they make and they put it out there which is fine, except that they don't taste the competition. If one comes on my course, I'll tell them to bring along something from a competitor and they'll show up with something quite unlike

theirs. Most are incapable of doing a comparative tasting. What they have to do is measure their cheeses against similar ones, so they know where they stand.'

Those with the intuitive skill, the ones who may be capable of producing a wonderful cheese that when tested blind wins top awards, are too often the ones who are struggling to survive because the makers have no sense of how to manage their 'Star'. Their failing goes beyond not studying the market and Juliet-the-agony-aunt at the end of a telephone has to listen to pleas for help with emptying a storeroom of unsold product. Where she can, she does. One distraught specialist called to tell her he was doing twenty-five farmers' markets a month. 'It was completely crazy. The more he did, the more he didn't sell. I advised him to cut back to ten or a dozen where he was doing well and spend more time concentrating on making his cheese that was suffering from neglect. He did. It got better and he sold more of it.'

Another of her bugbears is the names, verging on the silly or facetious that can destroy the image of a seriously good product, almost before it's off the ground. She cited 'Nannie's Nipple' (it's really Nibble), a goats' cheese made by Whitelake, an excellent Somerset dairy. 'Please,' she begged its maker. 'Change the name.' Of course there are the unlikely christened varieties that prove the exception, for instance, Stinking Bishop.

Most of the time, when she pulls the strings, she does it discreetly, tipping off a journalist about a promising newcomer, then contacting a few retailers to let them know that such-and-such is about to have some publicity. The newcomer receives an order. The magazine publishes its story and the retailer sells the product. As grey eminences go, Juliet is up with the best of them.

What she has never done is compromise her standards, always acting on her convictions, trusting her own judgement. One of the most sympathetic awards she created is 'The Cheese Lover's'. If she were not the lady running the show, she would be the perfect person to judge it.

Above: Retailing and gastrotourism combine on a sunny Cotswold morning.
Below: The accurate recording of the date on which a cheese was made is essential to managing the ripening process.
Opposite: Fourteen-pound rounds of cheese mature for a minimum of seven months in the store.

Mary Holbrook's Sleight-of-Hand

Sleight Farm (pronounced to rhyme with 'fate'), built of grey, weathered Bath Stone, clings to a steep Somerset hillside outside the village of Timsbury. By day, the skyline from its yard is filled with the first green outcrops of the Cotswold Hills. After dark, to the north-west, the orange glow of Bristol blurs the horizon. The house and outbuildings are surrounded by lush pasture left unploughed for over half a century, ideal for the motley herd of goats that graze it.

White, brown, black, flecked or parti-coloured, they reflect a cross-section of breeds: floppy-eared Roman-nosed Anglo-Nubians, short-coated Saanens, swart Alpines with white war-paint lines down their cheeks, stocky Boers and every kind of in-between hybrid. Collectively, they provide the milk that Mary Holbrook, a pioneer of Modern British cheesemakers, turns into pyramids of Tymsboro cheese.

She began thirty years ago, when Cheddar, Stilton and the other hard territorial cheeses were virtually the only ones being made in Britain, when imported Parmesan was sold ground up in cellophane packets, Camembert was 'that smelly French stuff' and Danish Blue was considered to be a Scandinavian exotic.

The two goats she kept on her parents' farm supplied the raw material for her earliest experiments. Her ambition then stretched to producing a little feta that she could sell to a wholefood store. She may have had the creamy complexion of a dairymaid – she still does – but that wasn't how she earned a living. A historian, she was curator of Bath's elegant Holburne Museum, caring for its collection of *objets d'art* and portraits by Old Masters such as Stubbs and Gainsborough.

As her enthusiasm for her hobby progressed, so did the size of her herd, as well as her aspirations to the extent that she decided to invite an Environmental Health Officer into the kitchen where she worked so that she could be sure she wasn't transgressing any basic hygiene regulations. Every surface, every utensil was spotless. The milk was impeccable. Unfortunately, a cat had crept into the scullery to watch proceedings from on top of the boiler. The public official suggested politely that Mary should consider moving to a purpose-built dairy.

On the European continent, goats are considered livestock like pigs, cattle or sheep. In Britain, where herds are few and far between, they have been treated more like pets. To build up her numbers, Mary had to experience the hardship of animals dying from mastitis or

Opposite: Mary Holbrook's goats are a mixture of breeds selected for the quality of their milk. This page: Mary breeds her own stock. Cheesemaking is seasonal, dependent on when the kids are born.

'Curious!'

pneumonia. Some she bought pined away because they couldn't adjust to the pecking order after being cosseted by private owners. To breed kids from them she had to borrow a Billy.

Meanwhile, as her experience and confidence grew, she started playing with a variety of cheeses both soft and hard. She went to France for a course in making Coulommiers, a Brie-like cheese. On another fact-finding mission to Tours in central France, she returned with the recipe for Valençay, a sawn-off pyramid-shaped cheese that, according to one legend, was invented to commemorate Napoleon's victories in Egypt. It became the direct inspiration for her own signature Tymsboro.

She hadn't yet considered giving up her day job, but by a twist of fate, her historical research opened the door that allowed her to commit herself fully to her passion. She had been travelling to London weekly to the Science Museum where she was preparing a catalogue of scientific instruments for publication and she always took a few cheeses for her friends and colleagues.

After work one day she stopped by Harrods Food Hall. While she was paying for some cheese she had purchased, the assistant who had served her noticed the cheeses already in her bag. When Mary explained that she had made them herself, the assistant advised her to fix up an appointment with the buyer, suggesting that he might be interested in taking some. This meeting led to a long, fruitful relationship with the London store and incidentally helped her make the decision to quit working as an academic.

It was a calculated risk. She had followed the advice to convert a small outbuilding into a dairy, but was still, like a French peasant, using pails for mixing milks and preparing the curds. However, she had also acquired a flock of Friesland sheep so she could develop a hard ewes' milk cheese. These were the size of a domestic colander for the simple reason that she emptied the coagulated milk into muslin-lined colanders to drain off the whey.

Her timing coincided with the first tentative attempts to protect existing traditional farmhouse cheeses, revive lost ones and invent new ones. A decade after the publication of the cult book *Small is Beautiful,* there was a reaction against agri-business and state-run institutions such as the Milk Marketing Board, which acted as a virtual monopoly, and an appreciation of buzz words like 'organic' or 'unpasteurised'. Randolph Hodgson at Neal's Yard Dairy was starting to source cottage industry cheeses like Mary's for its Covent Garden shop. The maverick wholesaler, James Aldridge, obsessive and passionate, was crisscrossing Britain buying the best cheeses he could find to sell on to a new generation of restaurants that didn't feel obliged to offer only French cheeses on their cheese boards.

If the impetus and original know-how for Tymsboro had owed more than a nod to France, it quickly developed its own identity. An obvious explanation is that the climate and the Somerset landscape differ from the Loire's. It's greener, wetter and cooler. The grass and herbs that goats eat affect the milk's taste, and as a result, especially if it isn't pasteurised, the cheese. The fact that the leys are mature, adds character in the same way that old vines can influence wine.

The season, too, plays a part. Her goats stop lactating as the winter approaches. Their kids are born before spring. Effectively this means that cheesemaking is only possible for eight or nine months. By keeping the herd indoors and controlling gestation, she could have continued throughout the year, but preferred instead to follow the natural cycle.

Like any other kind of recipe, making cheese requires the ability to follow a few simple, specific steps. In Tymsboro's case the previous night's and the morning's milks are mixed to a precise temperature. A bacterial starter is added to develop the lactic acid that helps it develop a characteristic flavour and texture. Next, a little animal rennet is stirred in that over some hours

53

coagulates the milk solids. Then the curd is ready to be ladled into lined moulds and left two to three days for the whey to drain. Once this has happened, the fresh cheeses are turned out, salted twice, then coated with a fine charcoal powder.

Simple as the process may seem, it's at the mercy of endless tiny variations. In a factory, where standardisation depends on the press of a button they can be dealt with. In Mary Holbrook's dairy, managing them hinges on a combination of craftsmanship and experience. She adds as little starter and rennet as she dare to let the natural bacteria in the milk act. This slows things down, producing a more complex-tasting cheese, just as bread made with less yeast takes longer to rise, but tastes better for it.

Because she doesn't pasteurise, she is, for good or ill, taking the presence of any bacteria in the milk on trust, believing that its effect will be beneficial. If, by some misfortune, they are attacked by phage, a virus that feeds on bacteria, and probably the most hated enemy of cheesemakers, a complete batch will be thrown out and fed to the pigs, because it won't be fit for human consumption.

However few cheeses she rejects now by comparison with her early experiments, she will never go through a season without having at least one 'failure' of this kind. She accepts it as an intrinsic part of dairying, a by-product of her refusal to compromise on the quality for which she strives.

To recognise and control the way in which her cheeses mature once they have been made calls

Opposite: Sleight Farm, halfway between Bristol and Bath, is on the edge of the Mendips.
This page: The cheese is related to the French Valençay from the Loire and is ripened longer than many English fresh cheeses.

for instinctive craftsmanship, born of years spent touching, smelling, looking. She has to turn each one so it develops evenly, control the temperature and the humidity of the room in which they ripen, to prevent them drying out or remaining too moist, so that when she sells them, they are smooth, creamy and clean-tasting.

When she goes to France nowadays, instead of being excited by cheeses that used to inspire her, she admits that she's often disappointed. Perhaps the French artisans are as good as they always have been: it's just she who has grown so much better.

One reason why she continues to be revered by her peers is that she keeps pushing back the boundaries of her knowledge. She describes herself as 'a great fiddler' always trying to improve. Sometimes, she says, she thinks she has found the

Above: A British Toggenburg goat at Sleight Farm. Opposite: As it ages the cheese takes on a dusky grey tinge reminiscent of the farm's grey stone walls.

answer to some detail that has been exercising her only, as in some endless quest, to realise that the solution leads to more questions. Her friend and dairymaid-in-chief, Phyllis, who has worked alongside her for over twenty years, knows the process inside-out, is totally competent, but hates any hint of experimentation.

Tymsboro (a seventeenth-century spelling of the village that Mary came across on an antique map) is one of many cheeses she has invented including Old Ford (a hard goats' cheese), Little Ryding, Tyning and Emlett (ewes' milk cheeses named after fields on her farm).

Until the infamous outbreak of foot-and-mouth in 2001 she had been producing as much or more Mendip (a ewes' milk cheese she had to abandon) from her 200-strong flock of Friesland ewes as she had from her goats. Although the disease never came closer than thirty miles, its impact was almost

enough to drive her out of sheep farming. For six months she found herself completely isolated. The regular rounds to farmers' markets in Bath and Bristol stopped dead. When, at last the disease was controlled she received an offer from a Cumbrian farmer to buy all her flock and she took it. It was, she confessed, touch and go whether the goats went with them.

Instead, she has carved out a new career for herself as a carer – of soft and mould-ripened cheeses. Every week she spends three days under the railway arches in Southwark, watching over the ripening rooms that Randolph Hodgson has built for Neal's Yard Dairy. That there are enough fine cheeses being made to keep her busy is largely down to the example she has given. Virtually self-taught, by trial and error, she is the unchallenged Godmother of Modern British goats' cheese.

Neal's Yard Dairy

Neal's Yard Dairy is the axis around which craft cheesemaking gyrates. The best cheeses are sold through its two London shops, in Covent Garden and at Borough Market, as well as overseas. The dairy's maturing and ripening rooms are unique. It's the centre of independent research into the methods adopted by the makers and a test-bed for what's being developed by them. At its core is the imposing guiding presence of Randolph Hodgson. He is both guardian of heritage and a stimulus to innovation. Without his energy, without his expert grasp of the complexities of dairy science and the mysteries that technologists haven't yet deciphered, British cheesemaking would be an anarchic, fragmented curiosity, dependent for its survival on a few cranky individuals, rather than a blossoming mini-industry with a sense both of its own worth and of where it's going.

Raised in Hong Kong, Randolph worked at the dairy when he was preparing for a degree in Food Science at London University, thinking that the experience of making fresh cheese and yoghurt would help him with his final exams. In 1979, after graduating, he stayed on: 'Most graduates would be going to work with major corporations in the food industry and I didn't want that.'

Not only did he remain here, but he bought the business from its previous owner. His early attempts at making cheese were, in his own words 'fairly embarrassing', but they prompted him to go out into the field in order to meet the handful of cheesemakers who knew what they were doing. They fell into two groups: those who were making 'territorials' such as Cheddar, Cheshire or Stilton, and the mavericks who were doing their own thing.

Until then Neal's Yard had only sold its own fresh cheese. Once he started bringing back others, and not necessarily fresh, that he had found on his study-travels, he discovered that he had little difficulty selling them. From a would-be cheesemaker, he transformed himself into a cheesemonger. By visiting and revisiting his suppliers, he learned to recognise, not only how a cheese might vary day to day, or season to season, but also from year to year. The changes, the lack of standardisation, were desirable; they were what distinguished the crafted product from the mass-produced one.

In 1989, when an unsympathetic Minister of Agriculture was about to legislate to ban the making of unpasteurised cheeses, he and fellow cheesemonger, James Aldridge, joined forces to found the Specialist Cheesemakers Association, a body that has punched above its weight in protecting the rights of a motley group of artisans, against the forces of bureaucracy and agribusiness.

On the subject of pasteurisation itself, Randolph has an unshakeable belief that a good cheese, made from milk that has been watched over in every detail, will be improved if the milk hasn't been heat-treated. That said, he admits that several cheeses he stocks, which he ranks among his favourites, have been pasteurised.

When he defends traditional methods, he always bases his argument on a scientific rationale rather than some folksy wish to preserve a technique because that's the way it was done in the 'good old days'. So he prefers the old starter cultures favoured by the Presidium Cheddar cheesemakers, such as Montgomery or Westcombe or Keen's (see p.82), because they are slow-acting and gentle, to the modern ones inoculated into the milk that act quickly and powerfully. He feels animal rennet gives better results than vegetarian ones, many of which are made from a genetically modified derivative to which he is opposed on principle. He would rather select a goats' or ewes' milk cheese that comes from a single herd, linked to the maker, because it will be more likely to have its own personality.

What has sustained him more, if possible, than the cheeses are the individuals behind them: 'The best thing about my work is mixing with the most eclectic group of people anyone could be dealing with, living in beautiful places.' At the other end of the chain, his customers represent, as a body, those who aren't prepared to compromise on the quality of the food they buy. They also act, he has discovered, as a barometer to whether a cheese he stocks is up to scratch or somewhere below it. For a period, sales of the only Stilton he kept dipped significantly because it was going through a bad patch.

One of the generalisations trotted out about the British taste for cheese, that there is a resistance to highly flavoured varieties, has no resonance at Neal's Yard, where the only reason anything is sold is because it does have a particular taste that identifies it. Randolph would qualify the description 'strong' that may too easily be applied to, say, blues or old cheddars. The term should not be synonymous with sharp, harsh, or acid flavours that have no other qualities other than the initial hit. The trick is to do things right at the right moments: to ensure that the milk is perfect, that the making is technically faultless, that the ripening, whether in the maker's

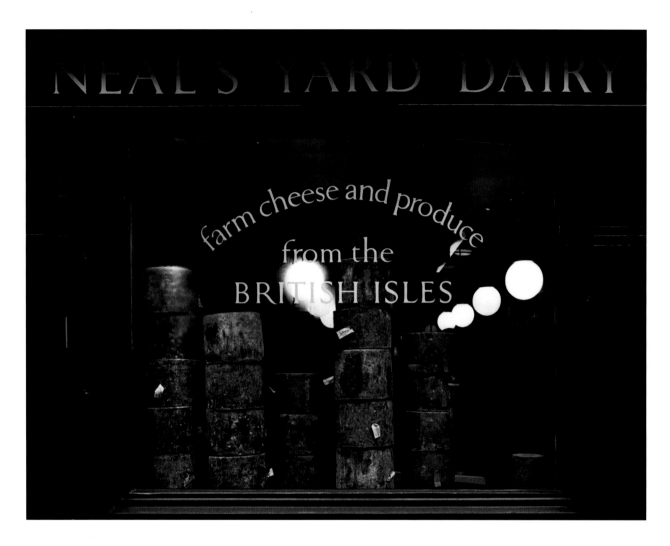

store or at Neal's Yard, is sympathetic, carried out to extract the maximum potential from the cheese.

Unquestionably, there has been a national leaning towards hard, aged varieties to the detriment of the soft. True; special mould-ripened ones such as Sharpham have been developed, but there are too many derivative Bries, too few of any real substance other than a pleasant butteriness allied to a smooth texture. In a series of soft cheese-ripening rooms, supervised by Mary Holbrook, who travels to London from Sleight Farm each week, Randolph has set about improving this perceived weakness. This is where experiments are carried out to produce a new breed of mould-ripened and washed-rind varieties which will stand comparison with the

Randolph Hodgson's original Covent Garden shop.

famous Camemberts, Bries and Vacherins. It's work in progress rather than 'job done', but he has created an environment where one of the most skilled British cheesemakers anywhere can have her head.

After twenty-five years' experience as the frontline apostle of British artisan cheese, Randolph enjoys the status of an honorary godfather. His judgement determines whether something is plain OK or special. A benevolent head of the family, he would probably express things differently. He would claim that ultimately, his customers take the final decision on his behalf. If that makes him a post-modern capitalist, so be it.

The recipe: When the curds have drained, sprinkle fine salt on, and spread with a feather. Place on a dry shelf turning them daily: when a fine white mould has covered them, they are fit to eat. Bath Cheese will demonstrate its ripeness, by spreading on bread as butter does with the aid of a knife.

John Prince
Agriculturalist 1908

Going Soft, Going Hard

Graham Padfield has the knack of portraying himself as a bucolic version of Basil Fawlty, hoping for a quiet life but convinced that invisible forces are conspiring against him. Among the longest-serving speciality cheesemakers, he has been living with his Bath Soft Cheese for well over a decade, never quite sure, one suspects, whether he or his cheeses have the upper hand. More recently he devised a new cheese 'looking like a football that has been sat upon', found an evocative name for it, Wyfe of Bath, and came to appreciate that perhaps there is a benevolent spirit watching over him after all.

He started making cheese for the kind of reasons that a traditional conservative dairy farmer with a large herd and a beautiful Georgian farmhouse might choose. Following the introduction of EU milk quotas, which meant that the amount of milk he produced was going to be capped, he realised he would have to come up with a way of increasing the value of what he had.

His family had owned the farm since 1904. In those days before subsidies existed, before bulk tankers collected the milk daily and a cheque for it

These pages: Bath soft cheese was popular in Edwardian times, vanished and was recreated by farmer Graham Padfield on his dairy farm at Kelston, two miles from the famous Georgian city.

arrived at the end of the month, his forebears would have supplied Bath and the surrounding towns with milk and cream. Any surplus during the summer would have been turned into cheese.

Euro grants – sweeteners that helped compensate farmers for lost milk revenue – were available and Graham decided he would use one to convert part of his dairy for cheesemaking. He approached the task with no more than a gut feeling that he didn't want to be another 'hard' man: 'There's no way a small person starting out can expect to make better cheddar than James Montgomery. What we thought we needed was a Brie-type cheese to sell well and it would be a license to print money.'

A visit to the local reference library, where he found an account of a long-lost Bath cheese, convinced him that he was on the right track. It described the method along with the instruction: 'When it is covered with a fine white mould … brush it with a feather.' Admiral Lord Nelson was allegedly sent some in 1801 by his father.

Above: When ripe, the cheese has a texture akin to Brie.
Opposite, clockwise from top left: Penicilliium-coated cheeses ripening;; Graham and friend; waiting for despatch.

A friend who had sold large-scale cheesemaking equipment handed him a recipe that was being used in factories and Graham began his experiments. On paper, the process looked simpler than a Delia Smith Spanish Omelette. In practice, it took him six months' tinkering with endless minor adjustments before he had one successful cheese. There followed a roller-coaster spell, making cheese in buckets, when he kept convincing himself that he had cracked it, only to find with the next batch that he hadn't.

He went on a fact-finding mission to the Scottish Borders where Bonchester, the only British farmhouse Camembert, was being made by John Curtis at Easter Weens Farm. There, only sixteen Jersey cows were being milked by hand, hardly the

money-spinning business Graham had imagined for himself. He sought advice from James Aldridge, who sniffed at his recipe. He moved from unpasteurised milk to thermised milk, a kind of gentle heat treatment.

By 1993, he had a square, soft, mould-ripened cheese, similar to a French Coulommier that he could, give or take a hiccup, achieve consistently.

After the difficult birth of Bath Soft Cheese, he quickly learned that it wasn't easy to delegate the dairy work by hiring staff who want to follow a routine: 'The point is that cheesemaking rewards total attention to detail. Most men are easy going and tend to do the minimum, whereas you need somebody who'll do the maximum.'

Soft cheese may not require months of ripening, but it is vulnerable from the moment the milk flows from the cow to when it has finished maturing. Un-glamorous though it is, cleaning a dairy every day may take longer than making the cheese. In 2006 he still suffers intermittent problems from the

These pages: When the Wyfe of Bath won a major award for Best New Cheese it turned round the fortunes of the farm.

fungal mould that the French call *poil de chat*, cat's fur, which can cover a white-moulded rind in charcoal whiskers. Even a small blot renders the cheese unsaleable.

Having devised something that looked good and tasted pretty good too, he faced the next hurdle, persuading enough sympathetic cheesemongers to buy it. Situated halfway between Bath and Bristol, he had two cities on his doorstep. Of the two, Bath is unique in attracting millions of tourists, who come to admire its Georgian architecture or visit the Roman Baths. It has always had a string of fashionable restaurants, but more relevant, it has two of the best, dedicated cheese shops in the country. The Fine Cheese Co. was in its infancy then, but a branch of the famous Jermyn Street shop, Paxton & Whitfield, encouraged him beyond

the normal limits of commercial practice, by agreeing to pay for the odd batch that it might have legitimately rejected.

Like other specialists Graham has created sister cheeses, Kelston Park and Bath Blue. But despite growing year on year, employing a skilled cheesemaker to manage the practicalities and a resting actor to help market his wares, setting up a stand outside Bath's famous Pump Room which sells up to £1,000 of his cheeses to the 'grockles' on Saturdays during the tourist season, he felt that his endeavours did little but keep one step ahead of awkward meetings with his bank manager.

That was before he and his cheesemaker James Ellis came up with the Wyfe of Bath. Named after one of the pilgrims in Chaucer's epic poem *The Canterbury Tales*, it's a cheese, which, depending on how you view it, is semi-hard or semi-soft. It isn't pressed but it's made in plastic colanders, like the

ones that Mary Holbrook used when she made her sheep's milk cheeses. It has a compact, lively texture, a kind of bounce to it and a clean, lightly acidic, buttery taste – like the eponymous lady herself.

Out of the blue, while Graham was in Wales, attending a Specialist Cheesemakers meeting, he learned that the supermarket giant Tesco had awarded it a prize for the 'Best Unknown Cheese' in Britain.

Graham admits that his actor-marketing-manager was probably overstating things when he announced to the press that the prize had saved Bath Soft Cheese Company from going down the pan, but it was a fair reflection of his intermittent disillusionment with the whole business of making cheeses, a market that has grown progressively more competitive for those who made mould-ripened Brie – or Camembert-style cheeses.

The supermarket order that went with the prize

doubled his turnover at a stroke. Of course, it could turn out to be a poisoned chalice. He who has the power to list, may also de-list, but for once, Graham could do worse than sit back and pat himself on the back. Even without the accolade and the revenue that the Wyfe of Bath will generate, he has created one of the most original and delicious cheeses, one that would make a worthy offering to Admiral Nelson were he still around to enjoy it.

The Fine Cheese Co.

It's very tempting to describe The Fine Cheese Co. in Bath as a kind of sweetie shop for grown-ups, where savoury cheeses replace mint humbugs, barley sugars and aniseed balls. So far as the comparison goes, it does reflect the sense of self-indulgence that is the essence of the shop. It may not have the gravitas of a Paxton & Whitfield, or the focus of Neal's Yard Dairy or the *sérieux* of a French *maître fromager*, but it catches to perfection the role cheese plays in modern British food culture. It's about style, enthusiasm, experiment and adventure.

If Ann-Marie Dyas, who owns it, were to look back over her shoulder, she would see herself starting out, at about the time chef Gary Rhodes was moving from the kitchens of a provincial hotel to the limelight of a television screen. It was a period, post the fashion for *nouvelle cuisine*, when knowing how to eat well was less about status and more about enjoyment.

Initially her ambition was to run the kind of deli where a customer could compose, if that was what they were looking to do, a perfect picnic. Now, it has become a cheese-inspired Dean & Deluca in miniature, a place that fits with the ethos of Bath as a chic international 'cityette' with its own sense of retail cool.

Along the way it has kept pace with the accelerating changes, both in scope and quality, of cheesemaking. Instead of showcasing the finest European cheeses, with a scattering of Anglo-curiosities added

on, as it did at first, Fine Cheese is all about picking the best home produce. Depending on the season, it will stock up to 100 British cheeses, the best it can find from a choice of 1,000-plus and increasing.

How Ann-Marie decides which ones to carry depends partly upon gut feeling and partly on commercial nous: 'If something tastes sensational, it's hard not to sell it, but obviously I'm looking to fill gaps. If someone were to come to me with a particularly nice young sheep's milk cheese, I'd lock the door and not let them leave, whereas it would be hard to get excited if someone brought in another Brie-style cows' milk cheese, because there's already Sharpham and Bath Soft. There are a lot of cheeses in that style.'

The speed with which specialist cheeses have multiplied makes her task easy in one sense, but it means that she has to act as an intermediary between them and customers who come into the shop with an appetite for cheese and only a modest experience of sampling them. Although most could name a dozen foreign types, they would struggle with British cheeses after running through a list of territorials.

Whereas she can become personally excited when a promising new cheesemaker such as Peter Humphries (once Graham Padfield's cheesemaker at Bath Soft Cheese) of Whitelake Cheese near Shepton Mallett starts producing imaginative washed-rind and moulded goats' cheeses with the unlikely names of Rachel and Nancy, she has to convince customers, to whom the names mean nothing, to buy them.

Because the habit of making and eating anything other than pressed cheeses died out in Britain, many new ones coming through owe more than a debt to established continental varieties. What's remarkable is that these invented 'after the school of' copies are always distinct from the originals. Be it the climate, milk, method or soil, they have their own personality. Fine Cheese customers aren't often aware of the link

Ann-Marie Dyas, the doyenne of the Bath Fine Cheese Co.

to say, a Pont L'Evêque or pecorino. They form attachments to a Keltic Gold or Stinking Bishop that are fresh and unaffected by preconceptions as to how such a cheese ought to be.

Because her shop doesn't have to support the weight of tradition, Ann-Marie has bolted on little extras to enhance the pleasures of cheese eating. Italians serve honey with Gorgonzola. The Spanish eat hard ewes' milk Manchego with *membrillo*, a quince paste. She has commissioned Barbara Moinet of Kitchen Garden Foods in Stroud to recreate the quince, damson and fig cheeses that were a popular accompaniment in Victorian days and there are herb-flavoured crackers and oatcakes to nibble with specific families of cheese: walnut oat with goats', fennel

crackers with washed rind, olive oil and sea salt for aged Parmesan or ewes' milk, 'red-hot chilli crackers' to eat with aged cheddar and old-fashioned charcoal biscuits that were once made at the Old Red House a celebrated Bath bakery.

A lot of the innovation is down to a flair for marketing pzazz – Ann-Marie, once worked in advertising. What she offers, though, is a lot more than the knack of presentation. She is the ideal ambassador for the disparate and sometimes isolated gaggle of small cheesemakers, because she simply loves cheese, talking about, selling it and, not least, eating it.

James Montgomery's Legendary Cheddar

Cadbury Castle may or may not have been the site of King Arthur's Camelot. 'Not' is probably the better call. The Saxon name tells us it's 'Cado's Fort', the domain of an obscure sixth-century king of Dumnomia, but a Tudor historian working for another monarch, Henry VIII, investigated the site and reported:

> 'At the very south ende of the chirch of South-Cadbyri standith Camallate, sumtyme a famose toun or castelle, upon a very torre or hill, wunderfully enstrengtheid of nature, to the which be 2. enteringes up by very stepe way: one by north est and another by south west... The people can telle nothing ther but that they have hard say that Arture much restorid [resorted] to Camalat.'

Hearsay, the proximity of Glastonbury Abbey – another key site in the Arthurian legend – and a desire to invest significance in a landmark rising 500 feet above the Somerset Levels has helped to reinforce the myth beyond any archaeological or historical support it has mustered.

Below its flattened hilltop, in the village of North Cadbury, three generations of the Montgomery family have been perpetuating a different kind of myth, one with more certainties than anything known about the King of the Britons, but one that has often been gilded, muddied or even traduced, the legendary cheddar cheese. They, and maybe two other Somerset cheesemakers, strive to make something that is in a direct linear descent from the sixteenth-century 'cheddars' that took two men to lift.

The cheddar myth has a strong emotional pull. Because the word itself has become a generic, adopted by cheesemaking around the world to describe a process, it would be so fitting were there some Golden Age to which its origins could be traced, instead of which there's a crowded, and to most people meaningless, babble of 'territorial', 'farmhouse', 'traditional', 'specially selected', 'aged', 'organic', 'vegetarian', 'low fat' cheeses offered for sale in an endless range of strengths from 'extra mild' to inedible 'strong'.

Montgomery's cheeses cut through the jargon of product positioning and placement. Like those made by farms in the days before there was any technological know-how to explain success or failure, his aren't standardised. They may vary day by day. Within a single batch, one may be outstanding another ordinary. One may have

developed the delicious 'nuttiness' that characterises the best cheddars after a year's maturation; another may still be improving after eighteen months. The variation is typical of what we might imagine to have happened in an idealised dairy where some cream-complexioned milkmaid sat on her milking stool pulling at cows' udders, except that, of course, it was never like that.

For a start, in Somerset most milking at the turn of the twentieth century still took place in the fields, with all the risks of contamination by muck that implied. Hygiene in the dairy was rarely better. An early 'scientific' report of a dairy that was well run, written when the risks to cheese by harmful bacteria were being recognised, commented on the presence of an earth-closet in the dairy. Cheesemaking was also seasonal, lasting from April to October.

Opposite: Montgomery Cheddar is matured for up to eighteen months.
Below: James Montgomery with crates used for potatoes on his Somerset farm.

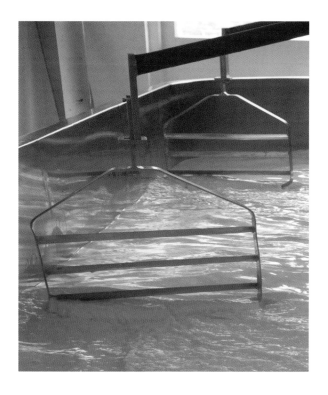

1. After it has formed, the curd is cut and stirred.

2. The drained curd is crumbly like gravel.

5. When the curd becomes firm it's ready to be cut into blocks of curd.

6. Cutting curd bricks is the unique cheddaring process.

3. Stacking the curd along the vat sides.

4. Resting the curd before cheddaring.

7. The 'cheddared' curd is stacked and rested.

8. The cheese is milled to form smaller chips.

The Great West Pennard Cheese

The Pennard men then built a cheese
The like was never seen
'Twas made and press'd and fit to please
Our gracious lady Queen!
And wedded to her royal love
May blessings on her fall,
And Pennard cheese at dinner prove
The best thing – after all!

West Country song

Soon after her accession in 1837, Queen Victoria received a gift from her loyal subjects of a gigantic brown loaf of bread. A group of farmers from West Pennard, a village between the towns of Glastonbury and Shepton Mallet, decided over a hogshead or three of cider that bread with no cheese 'weren't no fit fare fer Her Majesty' and formed a committee to produce a single cheddar grand enough to offer her.

A special octagonal mould three feet in diameter and press was built by a local blacksmith. A carpenter carved the royal coat of arms on a Spanish mahogany 'follower', used to stamp the cheese during pressing. The milk from 787 cows was collected to produce something short of 1,500 gallons, enough for a half-ton cheese. They were ready to go.

At 5 a.m. on Friday, 28 June 1839, a cannon was fired, church bells rang and the making of the cheese began at the farm of one George Naish with about twenty-five dairymaids in attendance. That evening there was a celebration at the West Pennard Inn with loyal toasts to Her Majesty and the dairywomen of the village.

The first hitch occurred days later when the cheese was thought to be properly pressed. It stuck to the vat and to the 'follower', so the experts put their heads together and decided that the curd contained too much whey, so the cheese was dismantled, milled, dried with cloths and pressed again. This seemed to do the trick because three months later it was put on public display for three days with proceeds going to the poor of the parish. By November, it was ready to move, with the help of sixteen

Many hundreds of farmers were making cheese with varying degrees of success. For some it was a prime cash crop on which their prosperity depended. For others, the odd cheese produced from a sudden surplus of milk represented little more than pin money. A gulf would have separated those with the highest reputation, whose cheeses were sent outside the county, from the rest, who may have carried their prize cheese to a local market.

And today we can have little concept of the scale of 'failure' with batches of milk that never curdled or cheddared properly, of cheeses tainted by anything from dirty milk to some weed on which the cattle had grazed. There was a rule of thumb that it took three acres of grazing to keep a cow whose milk would be dedicated to cheese. In an era when smallholding and small herds were the norm, when yields were lower and milk less rich, there were no agreed standards as to how much or little a cheese should weigh, how old it should be before it was ready to eat, or how it should be made. A very early Elizabethan reference to cheddar, describes it as 'being of such size as to take two men to lift it', but neither it nor the famous West Pennard cheese (see feature above) were typical. They are recorded labourers, from the dairy to a final ripening room in the house of John Dunkerton.

Victoria married Prince Albert in February 1840, when the villagers invited a party from nearby Ilminster to a celebratory viewing. At Whitsun, Dunkerton provided beverages for around 1,000 curious cheese-watchers. It wasn't until later in the year that it was officially described as 'ripe' and ready for delivery.

A deputation of three farmers decked themselves out in specially tailored suits and headed for Buckingham Palace. Her Majesty and her new consort received them graciously, but gave them to understand that the Queen preferred old cheese to new – What was she thinking of? It was already over eighteen months old – but if they would take the cheese back to where it came from and present it at an unspecified future date, she would give £100 to the poor of the parish.

The three farmers were delighted at the chance of a second brush with royalty and returned to West Pennard, suitably inflated. They became known about the village as the Marquis of Sticklinch, the Duke of Woodlands and Lord East Street, a humorous tribute to their enhanced status. It was planned to represent it for the expected royal christening.

At this stage the cheese saga turns bitter. First there was an attempt to vandalise it and it had to be protected by an iron cage. The village divided into factions. One group made a plaster cast of the cheese using the vat, took it to London and put it on show. A second faction, who had possession of the real cheese, also took it to London and exhibited it at the Egyptian Hall until the rival group took out an injunction preventing them doing so. A costly lawsuit followed, leaving both groups out of pocket, but with a ruling that the cheese might no longer be shown in the capital. In a peak, the yeoman 'Marquis', 'Duke' and 'Lord' took their cheese on a tour of Somerset towns, living high off the proceeds. It never reached the royal table. Instead, it ended up first on a farm in the hamlet of Sticklinch then, after the farmer's death, with the Duke of Woodlands, who had become landlord of the Old Down Inn. By the time anyone tasted the cheese it was probably rotten, but it was eaten, eventually, by pigs.

precisely because they were exceptional.

Nor is there any evidence that the cheese from around Cheddar Gorge, with which John, Lord Poulett tried to stock up in 1625 only to discover, 'They have grown in such esteem at Court that they are bespoken before they are made', was similar to what is eaten today. It's more likely that it wasn't. Over a century later, Somerset Cheese is described in *A Compleat Body of Husbandry* by Thomas Hale:

'This is a large rich cheese, named from the county where it is made. The bigness is a material article for I've seen the same cheese made smaller. What is singular is that there is butter worked into it which helps the mellowness.'

The method has similarities with cheddar:

'Rennet 30 minutes covered, break and press down the curd, separate the whey and when the curd has been well-worked with the hands, add three pounds of butter. This must be worked into the curd and a little salt sprinkled over it, then pressed.'

Once it has been made, Hale gives instructions for the cheese to be turned regularly, 'And every time carefully wiped'.

Another century went by before cheesemakers

Cheese is only as good as the milk from which it's made.

who managed the uncertainties of their craft to best effect, recognising subtle differences, hypersensitive to any warning signals from the cheese vat.

Like the stalactites in the Cheddar Gorge caves, Montgomery's cheese represents the culmination of the slow drip from centuries' experience. It's a cheese of fundamentally simple steps which begin, each one of them, with an unspoken personal guarantee: 'This is the best way we know how to …', which is something on another plane from the industrial dairy that sets itself a standard and takes pride in maintaining it.

What this means in practical terms is that James nurses a healthy relationship with each batch of cheese he makes, knowing that no two can be identical, that he isn't cloning, that he can't remain in total control: 'I don't want to worry whether we could do something so scientific that it produces the same cheese all the time.'

This isn't some Luddite refusal to accept change, nor is it founded on some whimsical notion of what may be authentically rustic. It's a recognition that accepting uncertainty, making it work in his favour, is the only way of ensuring that cheddars leaving his store will all have character and that the outstanding ones will be among the finest cheese of any kind being made in the world.

Relying entirely on milk from his own herd, it may seem that he is best equipped to control his raw material. What matters to him isn't the amount of fat and protein in the milk so much as their relationship to each other, where the latter acts as a kind of net and the former, its catch. The more fat is trapped, the more body the cheese will have. After twenty-five years' experience, he has learned that it takes no more than a flock of starlings raiding his cattle feed to change the milk's character and undermine his careful balancing act.

Apart from milk, there are only three ingredients in cheese, a starter, rennet and salt.

When the Somerset Cheese School investigated the use of 'starters' in 1897, its director, a chemist

started cutting up the blocks of curd after the whey had been drained from them and stacking them in the style that has come to be defined as 'cheddaring', but there was no concept then of what a starter culture was, because there was no appreciation of the invisible world inside the milk. If brushing the cheese with melted lard and binding it in cloth was recognised as best practice, it was far from universal. The best cheesemakers were those

Protected Designation of Origin
West Country Farmhouse Cheddar

/ 39°–40°C. The curds are cooled after being separated from the whey and are then cut into rectangular pieces. The curds go through a process of 'cheddaring' where the pieces are turned and stacked by hand on top of each other. After a process of 'milling' where the pieces are cut, salted and then mixed thoroughly, curd is put into moulds and mechanically pressed. After pressing the cheese is removed from the moulds, sealed, wrapped and stored to mature for at least nine months in the area.

Protected Designation of Origin Main Criteria:

Cylindrical or block-shaped firm cheese, creamy yellow in colour, made from cows' milk. Nutty, full-rounded flavour with a hint of sharpness achieved through natural maturing.

Area: Dorset, Somerset, Devon, Cornwall

The milk used to make the cheese comes from the cheesemakers' own herd and local farms in the designated area except in times of shortage when it also comes from the surrounding areas of Gloucestershire and Wiltshire.

After the addition of starter culture and rennet to the milk, to coagulate the milk and form a junket of curds and whey which are then cut and scalded at a temperature of around 103° – 106°F

Farms currently making PDO Cheddar:

A. J. & R. G. Barber Ltd
Alvis Bros Ltd
Ashley Chase Estate t/a Ford Farm
Cricketer Farm
Denhay Farms Ltd
F. A. W. Baker Kingston Farm Ltd
Farmhouse Cheesemakers Ltd
Gould, E. F. J. & Co.
H. G. Green (Cheesemakers) Ltd
J. A. & E. Montgomery Ltd
Longman Cheese Sales
Milton Westcombe Farms
Parkham Farms
R. L. Clapp & Son (Cheesemakers) Ltd
Tower Farms

Dr F .J. Lloyd, assured cheesemakers: 'I had come to the conclusion from my observations that inoculating the milk with a pure culture of the lactic acid bacillus would not insure a good cheese... the organism alone will not produce that nutty flavour which is so much sought after as being the essential characteristic of an excellent Cheddar cheese.'

So what is this 'starter' that he rejected and without which today's cheesemakers couldn't operate? It's a live bacteria culture producing the lactic acid that affects the taste, the texture and the moistness of a cheese. Just as bakers would

A Winter Salad with Montgomery's Cheese

This recipe was provided by Richard Guest, head chef at The Castle Hotel, Taunton, Somerset

Serves 4

100g Montgomery's Cheddar
1 small Cox's apple
Handful of black grapes
1 tsp Dijon mustard
1 tsp runny honey
1 tbs lemon juice
4 tbs Spanish olive oil (not a strong Italian one)
Salt
Mixed winter salad leaves
1 tbs pomegranate seeds

Cut the Cheddar in half. Slice shavings from one half and set aside. Cut the other half into small cubes. Core, quarter and slice the apple. Halve and seed the grapes. To make a dressing, mix the mustard, honey and lemon juice together. Whisk in the oil and season with salt. Toss the salad leaves with the dressing in a bowl and add the cubed cheese, apple and grapes. Toss again, so that everything is coated in the dressing. Arrange the salad on individual plates or in small salad bowls. Decorate each one with pomegranate seeds and pile the shaved cheddar on top.

keep back a piece of raw dough as a leaven to activate their bread from one day to the next, early cheesemakers, without any grasp of the science, retained a little whey or cream from a successful cheesemaking, known picturesquely as 'back-slopping', to mix with the next batch.

From being an optional extra and by its nature fallible, it was developed into a pure culture that has become an essential part of the recipe. With a century of food science behind them, starters come, metaphorically speaking, in many shapes and sizes. Cheesemakers tend to use them in blends, rather like a cook's bouquet garni, to create a special taste.

For James, it is critical that his strains of starter have been grown as though they were naturally occurring in his milk rather than developed as a flavour enhancer in a laboratory. He uses ones that were originally collected from dairies during the 1930s. Known as 'pint starters' because they are prepared in liquid pints, not envelopes of freeze-dried bacteria, they need constant care and must be re-inoculated regularly to remain vigorous. They are increasingly hard to come by and few other cheddar makers, including Keen's at Moorhayes Farm and Westcombe Dairy, both of which work with raw milk, still choose it.

The UK's Vegetarian Society succinctly describes what rennet is and what it does: 'Milk is coagulated

Clockwise from opposite above: Cylinders may look alike in the store ... but sampling with a cheese iron is necessary to see whether they make the grade.

by the addition of rennet. The active ingredient of rennet is the enzyme, chymosin (also known as rennin). The usual source of rennet is the stomach of slaughtered newly-born calves. Vegetarian cheeses are manufactured using rennet from either fungal or bacterial sources. Advances in genetic engineering processes means they may now also be made using chymosin produced by genetically altered micro-organisms.'

The society's pro-vegetarian rennet argument might run thus: why slaughter calves when a genetically engineered compound can achieve the same result? James answers: 'Early veggie rennet had a reputation for making cheeses more bitter.

That may no longer be so, but I'm so strongly against bitterness that I won't take the risk. Having looked at cheesemakers who use both, I'm sure that there's a more complex, more rounded flavour.'

At a moral level, he argues that half the cattle born are bulls. The lucky ones will be reared as steers for beef, the rest will have no value except as veal. Suppressing animal rennet wouldn't in any way alter their lot.

The way his cheddar is made on the farm hasn't changed in three generations. The diluted starter is left overnight in a sealed churn. When the previous evening's milk has been combined with the morning's milk the starter is mixed in and the rennet added. Left until it forms a junket, the soft curd is cut with mechanical harp knives, then it is scalded and stirred in the whey that has separated from it until the curd forms rubbery pea-sized lumps.

The whey is drained off and the compacting curd is stacked along the sides of the vat ready for

Above and below: Jersey Shield, produced with milk from his mother's pedigree herd, proves that Montgomery isn't hide-bound by tradition. Opposite: Portrait of a gentleman farmer in the Gainsborough style.

cheddaring. To do this it's cut into bricks, stacked and turned for up to an hour before being shredded through a blunt-edged 'peg mill' that will produce a more crumbly cheddar than those where the curd has been sliced. The chips are then salted before being packed in muslin-lined hoops. These moulds are laid end to end in a gang press and the cheeses are pressed to remove any residual whey. After a few hours, they are scalded to create a kind of skin that will prevent the cheeses from cracking and then pressed again.

Before being transferred to the storeroom, they are bandaged with lard-soaked muslin. The technique is one of those evolutionary accidents that can't be improved upon. The lard protects the inside of the cheese against invasion by moulds. By the time it has gone, consumed by bacteria, the inside of the cheese is protected.

During the aging process, the rind remains intact and it is never shrink-wrapped or treated in any way to aid moisture retention. A cheddar's weight can vary from fifty-five to seventy pounds, and may age from a minimum eleven months to two years.

Nurturing each one takes constant observation. It's as much a part of the process as managing the herd and making up the recipe. Things can and do go wrong. If the curd is too acid, it can develop into a hard-textured cheese lacking strength of flavour. A crack in the crust may be invaded by mould. Individual cheeses mature at

Above: Jersey Shield can be melted like the Savoyard raclette.
Opposite: Cadbury Parish Church.

different rates. They need tasting often to check how they are aging, bored into with a cheese iron that, like an apple-corer, removes a plug. As an *aide-mémoire* James writes notes for each test as a winemaker might: 'I talk a lot in terms of shape. Round is good. Creamy, fruity, nutty but *no ragged edges*. Ragged implies sharpness. I'll note *spikes* of rotting flavours when the fruitiness is past its best. Maybe once a year, I'll come

across a cheese where the fruitiness fades out immediately. Acidity masks flavour, so we've taken the decision to move away from acidic cheeses.'

Because cheddar is a generic, made all over the world, there was until recently no way, other than by tasting, of discriminating between one that had been hand-crafted on a Somerset farm and one that had been mass-produced in an American factory. This anomaly was partly dealt with by creating a Protected Designation of Origin (PDO) for West Country cheesemakers who make cheddar almost exclusively with milk from their own herds. It's part of a standard European Community scheme that defends hundreds of products from olive oils to chickens – though most people will associate it with wines. Thirteen farms belong to the scheme, a mere handful compared to the 400-plus cheddar makers who were active at the outbreak of the Second World War.

Montgomery's is a willing member of this exclusive club, but feels that it doesn't go far enough. The Slow Food Movement, founded in Italy in 1986, has grown into the most powerful international lobby for the defence of endangered produce and artisan foods. It has set up what it calls Presidia (from the Latin for a fort or garrison) for specifically threatened food. With the only two other Somerset dairies that produce unpasteurised cheddar (Keen's and Westcombe,) James, under the Slow Food umbrella, formed a Presidium that goes beyond the standards laid down for PDOs without the red tape, derogations and formalities of federalist schemes. It represents a line in the sand, commitment never to compromise.

Whether this is some quixotic Arthurian last stand against inevitable change or a glorious fight to revive a cheese that could still fail, James Montgomery is standing up for something he's justly proud, something that is unique.

Montgomery's Jersey Shield

During excavations in 1997 below the ramparts of Cadbury Castle a Bronze Age shield was discovered. Wafer thin, it was an object of ritual value, though pointless as a form of personal defence. Its origin, about 1,000BC, is evidence that the hill-fort was an important strategic centre 1,500 years before Arthur came here – if he ever did. When James Montgomery chose this artefact as an emblem for his Jersey Shield, he pitched on an ancient symbol to promote a cheese that breaks with many of the articles of faith for traditional cheddar makers and that was – oh yes – invented by two travelling Americans who had stopped by his farm.

The Montgomery farm has two separate dairy herds. Milk from the Jerseys, the special concern of James' mother who created it and built it up, has never been made into cheddar, because it doesn't make good cheddar. There is though, no reason, as new wave cheesemakers have shown, why it shouldn't make a good cheese.

Early in the new millennium, James was contacted by two young Americans who were touring Europe on a tandem as part of their research into Old World cheese. Would it be possible, they asked, to spend a fortnight on Montgomery's farm? James agreed but wondered how he was going to keep them occupied. He hit upon the idea of letting them make cheese.

For the fourteen days of their visit he allowed them to 'play with' a twenty-gallon vat of milk from his mother's Jerseys under a regime of limited supervision. 'None of us,' James recalled, 'had any idea how things would turn out.' He provided the steadying expertise. They experimented with recipes that would never have occurred to the cheddar maker such as salting the curd before the whey has drained off, initially a 'hit and miss affair', but one that gets the cheese into the mould with more whey left in it giving a softer, moister curd.

His guests' enthusiasm was catching: 'It triggered me to get off my backside and try something different.' After they had left he set about ripening the samples and making more. The Jersey Shield he eventually showed at the World Cheese Awards in 2001 won a Gold Medal. Looking like French mountain Tommes, it is made from raw milk and is at its best while quite young, at about four months old, though it does age. The curd has a springy texture and a very creamy mouth-feel that clings to the palate. You can try it for free if you travel First Class with British Airways.

This should have been the end of a small but satisfying success story about the birth of another modern British cheese. It does have one further twist to it. Jersey Shield was sent to Neal's Yard Dairy where the storeman, Bill Oglethorpe, used it for raclette on his Saturday Borough Market stall. Raclette is a fancy French word for what is often a bland melted cheese. But of course no Montgomery cheese could be accused of blandness and queues formed to buy the cheese when its aroma wafted through the market.

Meanwhile, Oglethorpe had also been 'playing' with Jersey Shield, washing it in a brine to vary its taste and texture. This hybrid cheese had an even more tantalising effect on the nostrils of London market-goers. All it lacked was a name. It was a problem that was vexing James until he was at Neal's Yard Dairy one day. He was discussing his dilemma with a buyer when Oglethorpe walked past. 'You know what you should call the cheese?' the buyer suggested, 'Ogle Shield'. The name has stuck, but because of its ties to Neal's Yard Dairy and the demand for it there, it's hard to find anywhere else.

Jersey Shield owes its existence to the resourcefulness of a couple of American visitors.

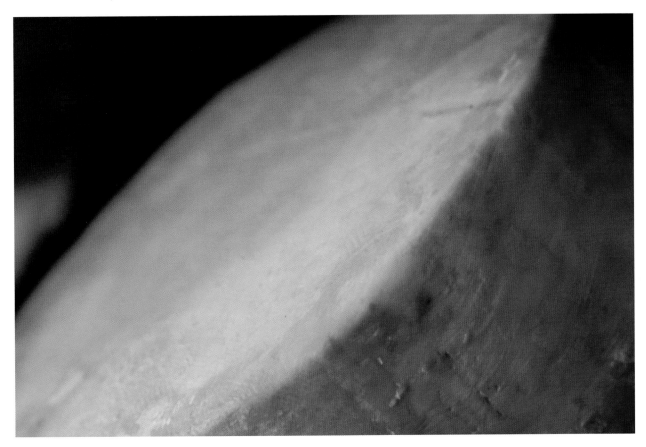

Somerset's Welsh Cheese

The Avalon Marshes, part of the Somerset Levels, stretch east from the Bristol Channel to Glastonbury. These wetland moors, broken into irregular rectangles by ditches, the landscape hedgeless, almost treeless, and houseless except for hamlets clustered on the higher ground above the winter flood levels, provide rich summer grazing for cattle – so much so that the name 'Somerset' itself, in Early English meaning 'land of the summer people', may have originated here. Cheddar Gorge lies on the fringe, between it and the Mendip Hills, a few miles from Wedmore.

Chris Duckett's parents and grandparents

farmed the Levels. His great-aunt, a famous cheesemaker, used to cycle seventeen miles from Mark to Cannington Agricultural College every day to learn how to make cheese when she was a girl. His grandfather on his mother's side was an important factor, supplying Sainsbury's when it

Above: Caerphilly-making flourished in the flat landscape of the Somerset Levels around Wedmore.
Opposite: Cheesemaker Phil Duckett moved the dairy from his Wedmore farmhouse to the Mendips.

was still a grocer's shop rather than a supermarket chain.

Growing up at Walnut Tree Farm, at Heath House a hamlet a mile or so from Wedmore, he picked up Caerphilly making by watching his mother and father. Since the 1960s he has nurtured and fought to preserve a farmhouse cheese that almost became extinct except as a characterless factory brand. If it were a sheep or a cow, his would still be rated a very rare and endangered breed.

Traditionally, Caerphilly was a Welsh cheese eaten by coal miners. They took chunks of it down the pits, wrapped in cabbage leaves according to one source, in their flat wallets according to another. It was tangy, salty, moist and digestible, an ideal food for men working in hot, humid, cramped conditions. Whether, as some believed, it prevented the debilitating lung diseases that affected them is open to question. At the turn of the twentieth century, when the Welsh valleys couldn't keep up with the demand,

Somerset dairy farmers started producing it. Their cheddar took a year to mature before they could sell it. Caerphilly was ready and paid for in days. At first, they shipped it across the Bristol Channel in the paddle-steamers that shuttled between Highbridge and Cardiff. Later, when the Highbridge port silted up, they switched to rail, packed on straw in open trucks.

Chris Duckett says that the locals never developed a taste for it: 'I don't know why. Perhaps they were too used to the cheddar.'

The Second World War closed down all Caerphilly making because the Ministry of Food believed, wrongly as it turned out, that it didn't keep. After the war, food shortages and rationing discouraged dairies on both sides of the border from starting up again. Some did though. Green's, one of the surviving farmhouse cheddar makers, did for a while; so did Barber's, another that was sending up to 1,000 Caerphillies a week across the border to Wales. When it lost the order, it stopped producing.

Tripper's Delight

Chris Duckett on a vanished cheese that his father used to make.

'Back in 1956, my father and a chap called Ralph Board started making a process cheese here [Walnut Tree Farm, Wedmore] and they bought a lot of unsaleable cheddar, stuff that was too acidic and stuff that was the other way and blended it all together. We had a little outfit where we made one pound and half pound cheese and they were sold in Cheddar Gorge in tinfoil with a green label round them.

'A lot of the cheese they bought was Canadian cheddar. It came in hexagonal wooden crates with slats all round the sides with two cheeses in it. Some of it wasn't bad. Ralph's father had made it before and during the War out at Chilton Polden.

He cooked it up; he had this big copper steam-jacketed thing that it was all mixed up in with paddles going round in it. They put it through a meat mincer, chucked it in the bowl, heated it and he had some sort of salt he mixed with it and boiled it all up and it was looking like custard then. We ran it out through this machine with a heated hopper on it, a nozzle on the bottom and a piston that went backwards and forwards over a rotating turntable. One of us would put the mould on and my father would keep the hopper filled up and Ralph Board would put a paper label on the top. Then it would be taken off, stacked and left to cool.'

This page: Caerphilly is a salty cheese, originally created for Welsh miners doing heavy manual work in the pits.

Others followed when the Milk Marketing Board offered them a guaranteed price for their milk, although they could have received a premium to continue cheesemaking. The Ducketts bucked the trend because they could still sell through the (now small) factoring business that Chris's uncle Edward was still running. They were though exceptional, soon the only farmhouse producing Caerphilly left in Britain.

Finding a market, Chris recalled, wasn't always easy: 'When trade was bad I went all round Weston-super-Mare trying to get people to stock some, but it never really caught on.'

In the late 1950s and into the '60s demand almost fizzled out. 'We were down to making

cheese one or two days a week because my uncle was having difficulty selling it, but the Greeks in London started buying it, because they said it was very much like one of their own ones.' It was the closest they could come to buying feta.

Not that the similarities between the two are obvious. Caerphilly comes from cows' not sheep's milk and it isn't swimming in brine for weeks. When fresh, though, it is white and open textured.

In Wales, it was nicknamed 'Crumbly', but Chris has never understood why: 'In my opinion,

87

These pages: The curd is piled into special hoops lined with muslin cheese cloths.

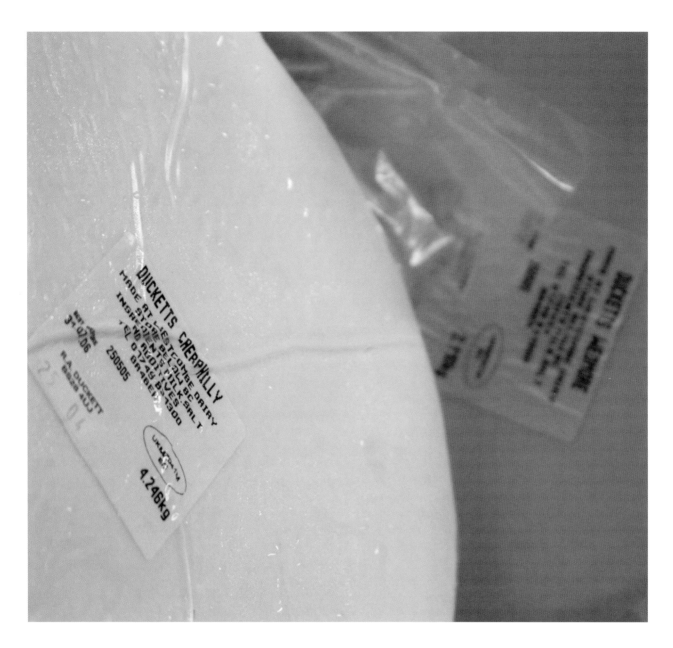

Opposite: Traditionally, hard cheeses are smeared with lard and then bound with muslin.
Above: The cheeses are vacuum-packed for extra protection before they leave the dairy.

it's a bad cheese if it is like that and I can't see how it could have acquired that name.'

The reason could be more to do with the way it's made. After curdling the full-cream milk with rennet, the cheesemaker cuts the curds into small gobbets so that the whey can drain off before pressing.

Maybe these outsize 'crumbs' explain the myth. Or possibly the earliest homemade Caerphilly was more like compacted cottage cheese.

The authentic version has a smooth open texture. It's fresher and moister than most other British hard cheeses. One reason why the early Somerset dairies took to it was that the recipe gave them more cheese for their milk than cheddar. Wheel-shaped, weighing eight to nine pounds (though Chris makes a smaller cheese, too), it has a distinctive ridge running round the outside formed

91

by a loose metal collar fitting inside the hoop in which the cheeses are packed and pressed.

A day's brining followed by a few days drying out and it's ready to eat. It tastes of fresh, faintly lemony, salty curd. It's exactly what miners would have expected and enjoyed in Victorian times.

Chris picked up the tricks of Caerphilly by helping his parents. There were no lessons other than experience. One day his parents decided they deserved a holiday, so they appointed him to take over while they were away. When they retired, he just slipped into their boots.

What turned things around for the Ducketts was the advent of the speciality cheese movement. Patrick Rance, a monocled ex-army major with a cheese shop in the Thames Valley called Wells Stores was attracting attention by comparing British territorial cheese made by the giant creameries unfavourably with those that were hand-crafted on farms. Fresh out of university a young Randolph Hodgson was embarking on his Neal's Yard adventure. Chris remembered him arriving at the farm in a battered blue Toyota van: 'He came along with shoulder-length hair and earrings and father said: 'Don't let him go with the cheeses until you have a cheque off him.'

It had never occurred to the Ducketts to age their cheeses, but it did to Randolph. He noticed that some Caerphilly carelessly left in a cardboard box at a Soho grocery was developing a rind.

He decided to experiment. Now he matures all of his this way in the cellars at his Neal's Yard Dairy warehouse. After eight weeks they develop a noticeable rind. The texture near the surface dries, but the middle stays moist. Meanwhile, the fresh curd mellows. Aged Caerphilly is less of a working-man's pick-me-up, more of a candidate for Gordon Ramsay's cheeseboard. The anecdote has an apocryphal ring to it, because in Wales, during the nineteenth century Caerphilly was

sometimes allowed to mature.

The third mover and shaker was James Aldridge, who scoured the country to find new British cheeses as well as the scant remaining producers of traditional ones. He was fascinated by the technology, especially the ripening process, as much as by the taste and wanted to create his own washed-rind cheese, something nobody else in Britain was attempting. He approached the Ducketts, asking them to supply him with miniature cheeses that he could take away and transform. By treating the surface with *Brevibacterium linens* and washing the cheese in brine to create a pinkish almost sticky surface, he invented the pungent Tornegus that is closely related to Pont L'Evêque. According to Chris, Aldridge's special ingredient was Kentish wine, included in the final wash: 'He used to say he drank more than he put on the cheese.'

The two men became close friends and, in 1998, they suffered the worst fate that can happen to any farmhouse maker, when a single case of the food-poisoning organism E. coli was laid at the Ducketts' door. A twelve-year-old boy had been admitted to a Taunton hospital. It was established that he had been infected by eating a piece of Wedmore cheese, a chive-flavoured Caerphilly made at Walnut Tree Farm. The investigators identified ten pieces of contaminated cheese, all made at Walnut Tree Farm on the same day. But they found no traces of contamination in the milk, nor in the dairy. There were no other reported cases of food poisoning. Nor were there any problems with Caerphillies or Wedmores produced on other days.

The storm might have blown over, except for a cruel twist. A month later Chris' Environmental Health Officer contacted him with a tip that there would be a hearing the next day at which it would be recommended that his cheese would be passed fit with the exception of a precautionary ban twenty-four hours either side of the day on which the rogue bug had entered the food chain.

That same morning, the officer rang to tell him a new positive sample had been traced to a Wells wholefood store. When, he asked, had Chris made it? Chris responded that it came from a later batch than the one implicated in the child's illness. It was enough for the authorities to condemn all the cheese and impose a temporary ban on all sales of Caerphilly, Wedmore and Tornegus under an Emergency Control Order.

What Chris only discovered later was that the sample had not come from the shop in question. It was a case of mistaken identity. The Wells store owned a sister deli in the town. When the testing was done, cheeses from both had been put together under the same trading name. The cheese with the E. coli trace had also belonged to the earlier and only affected batch. He had in fact almost been ruined because of a product being sold to a shop he didn't know he was supplying and by a flawed investigation.

At the time the *New Statesman*, in an article defending Chris Duckett, wrote: 'We are not only destroying a classic English cheese – we are bragging about it.'

For James Aldridge and his Tornegus there was a gross failure of natural justice. He lost ten weeks' worth of stock maturing in his cheese store. Despite his having had it tested, despite it being cleared, the whole lot was condemned with no option of compensation. The government escaped liability by claiming that the condemned cheese was Duckett's Caerphilly.

It could have broken Chris Duckett, but he has continued making Caerphilly, though no longer at Walnut Tree Farm. Three years ago, he shut the doors of his dairy, packed his vats, his moulds and his press and moved them to Westcombe Dairy, in the Mendip Hills, which he rents from cheddar maker Richard Calver. He hopes that his landlord may find a cheesemaker to take over from him when he retires. Is his Caerphilly as good as it

was? Good enough to continue winning Gold at the Cheese Awards, but it isn't the same. He notices that the curd has changed. It's a little firmer, maybe due to a new milk source, maybe to the microclimate or the way the air circulates in the dairy. It's one of those imponderables that are part of the cheese mystery.

In Wales Caerphilly is being made again. Todd Trethowan, who worked at Neal's Yard, learned how to make Caerphilly the Duckett way by working alongside him, before setting up his own dairy at Gorwydd Farm, near Lampeter. He has carried the ripening a stage further, keeping his cheese up to three months before releasing it. It may not be the kind of fresh young curd cheese for wrapping in cabbage leaves and taking down the pit, but Chris Duckett is happy to give it the thumbs up.

Chris is concerned, though, about his own cheese's future should he ever he decide to retire. Now over sixty, he is the last maker in the region with the expertise, but has found no one to whom he can pass it on. Ideally, it should be preserved as part of the conservation work on the Somerset Levels. Environmentalists have ongoing projects to preserve the peat, the withies and the wildlife of the wetlands, why not another unique part of its heritage, Caerphilly?

James Aldridge

James Aldridge was both a hero and a martyr in the realm of British cheese – and a more unlikely one it would be hard to imagine. Whisky drinking, a heavy smoker, anxious, intense, straight talking, straight dealing, he was totally absorbed by his work. Nothing in his past suggested him for the role. Having injured his back, he was an out-of-work scaffolder when he met Pat Robinson running a Southampton shop that stocked bacon and cheddar from the now defunct Horlicks creamery in Ilminster.

The couple opened a cheese shop in Beckenham High Street, stocking, for the most part, British cheeses in the late 1970s. Not content to stay behind a counter, he travelled the country, meeting the established Stilton, Cheddar and Cheshire makers, but also sniffing out the pioneers such as Robin Congdon or Mary Holbrook. Anybody who was trying to make cheese then, was likely to receive a visit. Always hands-on, he touched, he smelled, he tasted and, as he gained in experience, he was able to advise newcomers. Generous with his praise, he often bought promising cheeses, knowing that he might not be able to sell them.

There was no ready-made culture to support the new cheesemakers, but James was astute enough to persuade chefs, especially those in fashionable country house hotels to give untried Beenleigh Blue or Sharpham a chance, or to rediscover unpasteurised Stilton or Montgomery Cheddar. Gary Rhodes, as a chef at the Castle Hotel in Taunton, would have discovered many of the better British cheeses thanks to James.

Chris Duckett's father Phil, farming on the Somerset Levels, began to supply Caerphilly, a young, then unpasteurised hard cheese. James collected it and took it back to his storeroom, a converted walk-in fridge and left it on shelves adjacent to some Colston Bassett Stilton. Blue Roquefort penicillin isn't the only flavouring agent in it. *Brevibacterium linens*, naturally occurring on the crusty Stilton rind was being transmitted to the Caerphilly, altering its character. James had been looking to do some cheesemaking on his own account.

He guessed that by smearing linens on smaller, made-to-order Duckett cheeses daily, he would be able to incubate it until it ripened into something quite different. He wasn't playing with an untried principle. Belgian Limburger and French Munster are both inoculated with the bacterium that produces a sticky outer coat with a slightly springy, smooth curd. To add a little extra mystique, following the continental ploy of washing rinds, he washed the cheeses in a little Penshurst, white wine from Kent.

The name he came up for it, inspired by Glastonbury Tor, was Tornegus. From a cheesemonger, its immediate success converted him into a professional cheesemaker. He closed the shop and built himself a dairy at Godstone, Surrey. By that time he had been elected the first British *maître fromager* by the French Guild of Cheesemongers. His cheeses were flying first class around the world on major airline menus. He was admired as a guru by the new breed of cheesemakers.

One day in 1998 a boy was admitted to Taunton hospital suffering from E. coli poisoning after eating some Duckett's cheese. It was an incident that nearly ruined Chris Duckett, and for James the consequences were equally traumatic.

Within days the Department of Health invoked the 1990 Food Safety Act and ordered James to destroy two months' stock of ripening Tornegus, even though it had been found to be bug-free. With no right to compensation he found himself facing bankruptcy, very angry and on the attack.

> **'You can start off with the same ingredients,' says James Aldridge. 'The same milk, from the same cow, milked on the same day. What happens to that milk depends on the enzyme action, which creates flavours, aromas, different acidity levels, and so on. Those enzymes are from bacteria, and by pasteurising you kill off all the bacteria. With pasteurised milk, the enzymes just aren't there. It makes bland cheese.'**
>
> **Extract from an interview in Food Illustrated, July 1999.**

The late James Aldridge examines a Beenleigh Blue cheese on a buying trip in 1985.

He sued in the High Court and won his case against the Health Minister, who was found to have acted for no better reason than 'administrative convenience'. Six months later the decision was reversed by the Court of Appeal in a verdict that infuriated small producers across the country. The judgement was debated in the House of Lords, which concluded that though the letter of the law had been upheld, James had suffered a miscarriage of 'natural justice'. He wasn't entitled to compensation, because the cheeses in his store were condemned for being Duckett's Caerphilly rather than Tornegus.

James never came to terms with his sense of grievance. When he died of cancer two years later, aged 61, in 2001, there was a real sense that this highly-strung cheese artist had lost the will to live. It could have been the end of Tornegus, except that Pat continued making it, still receiving Caerphilly from Chris Duckett every week. She has also become a reputed innovator in her own right. Celtic Promise, another washed-rind cheese, made at Godstone, has been one of the most highly regarded cheeses in Britain since she invented the recipe. It is, though, washed in cider.

Where the Buffalo Roam

It would take a pretty good map-reader to locate Frances Wood's farm in the hamlet of Upper Alham. Tucked into a wet, claustrophobic rift valley in the Mendip Hills, only two or three miles from the cheddar maker Westcombe Dairy, it could be in another part of the country. The farmhouse itself, long and narrow, must have been built in the eighteenth century and extended by a Victorian farmer. Bought by an urban émigré, it could be converted into the epitome of country living. Instead, a working farmhouse, its interior forms a row of low-ceilinged, dark rooms: the old dairy leads to a busy kitchen, through to an office and, at the far

end, a living room filled with heirlooms that would attract the covetousness of the gypsy knockers who doorstep farmers in search of antiques.

In the yard, a modern refrigerated lorry (Frances has an HGV licence) contrasts with a 'dead' van that might once have hawked ice-creams. The cowsheds opposite the house are neat. It's only by going up close and peering in that one notices that the black-coated livestock standing on a thick bed of clean straw aren't cows but young water buffalo.

During the Middle Ages, probably as a result of the crusades, there was an attempt to introduce buffaloes to Britain from the Near East. It failed

Opposite: Buffaloes imported from Romania form the basis of the Alham Wood herd.
Right: Frances Wood began cheesemaking to help cope with bereavement.

here and in France, too. In Italy, it was a different story. They were already known in Lombardy at the end of the sixth century and, although they weren't generally farmed, they must have spread slowly through the country because fresh buffalo cheese was familiar to Florentines in the early Renaissance and the first written record of mozzarella was passed down by Bartolomeo Scappi, cook to Pope Pius V, in 1571.

Not your average cheesemaker, if such a person exists, Frances Wood couldn't claim to have had more than a sketchy notion of cheesemaking when she flew to Romania, took a train to Cluj in Transylvania and returned to Somerset with enough buffaloes to start her own herd. She could, though, confidently assert that she has milkmaid genes. A century ago, her grandmother, who ran 'Natty' Rothschild's dairy on his estate at Tring, won a cheesemaking cup at the National Dairy Show in London's Royal Agricultural Hall.

It was a television programme on Italian cookery presented by Antonio Carluccio that planted the idea of switching a part of her dairy farm to buffaloes. A little research in a textbook on tropical agriculture, which explained how the Asian buffalo species provided milk meat in abundance, that it was resistant to disease and easily managed, added to her growing fascination. Confirmation from the then Ministry of Agriculture that buffalo milk was not subject to milk quotas, turned fantasy into possibility. Commercially, buffaloes seem the perfect cheese-producing machine, since a gallon yields twice the weight of cows' milk. The fact that Germany was already importing them from outside the EU meant that there could be no objection to her bringing them into the UK.

Finally, she learnt that one other British farmer had already put in motion plans to import them.

In wider Europe, the two countries with large stocks were Romania and Bulgaria, both adjusting to the downfall of communist regimes. Of these, Bulgaria reputedly had better animals, but had problems with foot-and-mouth disease. So she chose Romania.

She might never have gone had it not been for her husband's death from cancer. During his life they had struggled to make ends meet on their dairy farm. Widowed she needed to do something radical that would take her mind off her loss. Despite the advice from friends and physicians not to make any major decisions, she took the plunge: 'I did it more as an act of kindness to take me out of myself.'

Arriving in Romania, she was chaperoned by a Professor Constantine Velea from Babes-Bolyai University, Cluj, who had written the standard work on buffaloes during the regime of the communist dictator, Nicolae Ceausescu. Visiting dismantled collective farms, she found that the animals' condition, especially in the long, cold winter, was affected by a poor diet of meadow hay and maize stalks, that they weren't significantly harder to manage than cattle and that they were resistant to disease. She was taught to judge a buffalo by its horns: size matters, the smaller the better. To her surprise, she noticed how, in spite of their being uniformly black their faces were easily recognisable from each other. Finally, she was informed that they live longer than cattle. Twenty years is considered quite normal.

Picking one here, one there, she returned to Britain having placed orders for twenty-six cows, eleven of which were in calf and a bull that had been selected by the professor. Shipped overland, they cost her less than £1,000 each.

While waiting for them to arrive, be quarantined and settle in, Frances started to practise on Arthur. This wasn't an unfortunate surrogate cow, but the name she gave her first cheese, produced from a small flock of ewes on the farm. 'We had a little stand and the assistant herdsman used to hold the things while I milked them into the milking pail, dashed indoors with it, strained it, shoved it in the fridge and then when I'd got enough I used to make some cheeses, one or two a week on the Aga.' She kept the cheeses in her living room on a table. Sometimes they passed muster. Sometimes filled with gases, they 'blew'. This doesn't mean they exploded, more

Opposite: Junas, a hard cheese, was named after the farm's boss buffalo cow.
Right and overleaf: Iambors, a younger fresher cheese, was named after the farm's original buffalo bull.

imploded, causing rents, gashes and gaping in the curd. In style, the cheese was a cross between Italian pecorino and Spanish Manchego, but the experience proved valuable when she switched to her rugged Romanian ruminants.

Eventually they arrived via Holland, having crossed Europe without any harm. They were quarantined for a fortnight in some disused buildings on a nearby farm, and walked the final mile down the lane to their new home.

They were ready to provide milk, but Frances hadn't turned herself into an expert dairymaid overnight. 'I had an old railway wagon and that was kitted out for cheesemaking. I had a couple of old custard boilers and the first thing that happened was I burnt one out and it had to be altered pretty quickly and we started making cheese.'

She persevered with an improving Arthur, while, figuratively speaking, dipping her toes into her buffalo milk. With hindsight she regrets her decision not to go straight for mozzarella, given its current popularity with the Jamie Oliver generation. Her argument with herself was that she had no customers. It was difficult to produce properly. It didn't keep. If she didn't sell it sharpish, it would be wasted.

Her preferred alternative, Junas, named after the boss buffalo cow, was a kissing cousin of Arthur, a hardish, matured and a keeping cheese. The theory might have justified itself, except that Frances lacked the skills of her prizewinning granny. In setting her initial cash-flow projections, she had pencilled £20,000 of cheese sales, balanced by a £20,000 salary for a cheesemaker. In fact, neither figure materialised.

By hiring a professional maker who had worked for the traditional cheddar specialist, Longman, by doubling the size of the vat and by relocating from the wagon to the farmhouse she turned potential disaster into potential.

As well as the Junas, she had embarked on a Romanian cheese Telemea, that is similar to feta when made from ewes', but smoother fashioned from buffalo milk. Frances christened it Iambors, after her bull. A brined cheese, it ought to be relatively simple to reproduce. It can though have a will of its own, the curd playing tricks that can throw trained pros.

eaten straightaway or left until the inside runs.

Her unpasteurised Junas, as it's intended to be, does share common points with aged Manchego. It has a firm white curd – buffalo milk always produces chalk-white cheese – with plenty of body. It's quite spicy, too. It also, quite rarely, probably when the fat levels are high, can develop into a powerful mouth-filling surprise, smooth as a Gorgonzola without any blueing, weird, unexpected and to those who enjoy a bit of bite, a treat.

Frances also takes to market hardened, almost blackened or discoloured Junas, ugly chunks that to the eye look rotten. Perhaps, that is what they are, but once the rind has been pared away the meat of the cheese, though strong, tastes neither bitter nor tainted. She isn't exploiting her customers' gullibility, because she keeps a similar wedge on her own kitchen table.

What makes Alham Wood Cheeses so attractive is that it represents work in progress rather than the finished item. It's the complete antithesis to a Daylesford or Curworthy, where the rigour of the cheesemaker has the task in hand under control. Frances' are unpredictable, on the edge. She goes her own way.

That independence extends to her approach to selling. Where many of the artisan cheesemakers are fighting to gain an entrée to Neal's Yard Dairy, Paxton & Whitfield and luxury food halls, or alternatively to sew up deals with the handful of wholesalers who act as the go-betweens or pitch for a listing with a supermarket, she has by-passed the official channels, cut out the middlemen. She has also not spread her net over the provincial farmers' markets. Rather, with a concentrated panache, she directs most of her resources to stalls in London markets. At weekends, when the working population goes out to spend its discretionary income, they can find Junas and Iambors at Islington, Pimlico, Notting Hill, Dulwich, Chiswick, Wimbledon and half a dozen

Once she had cracked the reliability challenge, Frances had a unique, versatile cheese that altered character as it aged. Part of its taste comes from the brine. Like the old Wiltshire bacon curers who never discarded their pickle, she keeps hers going, simply adding water or whey and salt to keep it at the correct strength.

At its freshest, Iambors has a supple but smooth texture that matches a sweetish milky taste. In its own way, it's as suited to Mediterranean salads as either feta or mozzarella. Left, for a week or so, it becomes slightly pasty, spreadable, and its flavour goes up a notch. There are two sizes: the larger big enough to slice that is sold by the weight; the smaller as a cylinder half the diameter of a Camembert and twice the depth. Kept back for a month or longer, it develops a natural bloom, effectively transforming itself into a mould-ripened cheese that can be either

*Right: Cascaval is made in Maltese hoops
supplied by an ex-Times cookery writer.
Below: Cheeses float in brine.*

other venues. For the rest, she admits that she is
one of the many who owe a debt to Juliet
Harbutt for directing her to new clients when
times have been hard.

The barrow-boy formula suits the cheese and its
originator. The approach has allowed her to
construct, if not pay for, a new dairy behind the
farmhouse. It comes fully equipped with a
Romanian cheesemaker – actually he's a qualified
food technologist, but who's splitting hairs?

If she had been brought up in the city, rather
than on a farm, Frances would probably have
matured into an entrepreneur. As it is she is
always trying out new schemes. It might be
setting up school visits to see her buffalo, or
developing a butchery sideline, or making meat

pies, or branching out into the clotted cream,
known as *kaimak* in Turkey, or perfecting a
ricotta recipe. She has new cheeses in the
pipeline. Frances Bissell, for years *The Times*
cookery writer, gave her some miniature
perforated moulds that she had brought back
from Malta. All she needs is a successful Maltese
cheese to put in them. Her prototype Cascaval, a
Romanian rip-off from the Italian Caciocavallo, a
semi-hard, that's shaped like a teardrop, is
coming soon to a market near you.

Her daughter Grainne has taken over as the
farm's herdsman. Mother and daughter have come
to love their buffaloes which they describe as
'more intelligent' than cows, more responsive to
the sound of their voices. Iambors has gone. A
new bull is on the way from Romania. As soon as
he arrives and she has found a name for him, she'll
probably be asking her cheesemaker to invent a
new cheese in his honour.

Fresh from the Rose Garden

Wiltshire is or was a region of pig farming, of bacon and the lacquered Bradenham ham. Cross Salisbury Plain by rail and you may still catch a glimpse of hogs rootling outside the corrugated huts that house them. It hasn't been thought of as a cheese-producing county, not since Daniel Defoe visited it on one of his tours around Britain and discovered that the county was exporting its own 'Single Gloucester' along the Thames to London.

The jigsaw puzzle of regional foods that places beef in Hereford, mutton on the South Downs, cream in Devon and cider in Somerset has long since ceased to have any meaning, so it isn't surprising, that after a twentieth century when no cheese was produced in Wiltshire, three good ones exist within ten miles of each other and within twenty minutes' drive of Salisbury. At Redlynch, Loosehanger Farms produces some fancy flavoured cheeses and a blue, Old Sarum. In the next village, Landford, excellent aged Gouda is produced at Lyburn Farm.

And then, at the other end of the village, facing the main road there is Rosary. Next door to a garage on the A36, it's easy to miss. The house, a little way back from the road is of red brick. It stands on a two-acre plot of land as unkempt at

Opposite: Chris and Claire Moody threw off the security of working in Southampton General Hospital to make Rosary.
Right and below: The couple didn't like French goats' cheese, so they set out to make it to a recipe they enjoyed eating themselves.

the front as it is at the back. According to Chris Moody whose mother was born here, his grandmother had made a small rose garden at the rear, which accounts for the name.

If it's long gone, that's no reason to charge either Chris or his wife Claire with laziness. Together they have laboured industriously to develop a goats' cheese that's fresh as a daisy.

As a child Chris had spent school holidays helping out on a farm. He had loved it. It's a shade ironical, then that he should have spent twenty-one years in Southampton General Hospital, toiling as a microbiologist in the immunology department. This is where he met and married Claire, a chemist. Both of them wanted out. Neither of them had saved a penny. So, when they moved into Rosary, they decided to rear pigs in their spare time, financing themselves through their day jobs. They dreamed that they might be able to quit their posts and reinvent themselves as smallholders. If anywhere, it should have paid off in Wiltshire.

In fact their bright idea backfired. Every penny of their salaries was spent on pay day, housing and feeding their large whites. Chris' eyes were soon opened: 'Just as I was starting, pig farming grew commercial. The animals were treated horribly, kept on slats, in crates and not the way I would have liked to keep them. But it pushed down the price. Before it would have been possible to make a modest living on a smallholding. It no longer was.'

The bacon had to go. It left a gap in their lives that was about to be filled by goats. Claire was listening to a programme on BBC radio, 'A Small Country Living', maybe the same one that inspired

Annette Lee at Woolsery (see p.119), that suggested they were very nice creatures and profitable, too. Chris didn't need much convincing.

While continuing to be employed by the hospital, he managed to fit in a course on goat-keeping at Sparsholt where he learned how to adapt the husbandry skills he had acquired with his pigs. Having transformed their piggery into a goatery, Chris and Claire went in search of livestock. The kids they bought grew. They produced milk and, as Radio 4 had promised, they were able to find buyers.

Their prize customer was a Greek, living in Hampshire, who was possibly the first artisan making feta and haloumi. His little business folded almost overnight when listeria was traced to his cheese and he had the national press camped on his doorstep. Undeterred by the setback, armed with the certainty that they had more than enough

scientific knowledge to prevent their milk from becoming a health hazard, Chris and Claire determined to produce cheese themselves.

Neither of them had ever been across the Channel, nor had they ever eaten goats' cheese, so as a basic piece of research they dropped by a small deli to buy some. Chris wasn't impressed: 'The ones we tried were horrible and we were thinking, "we've got to make our living out of this".'

It was, he conceded, just bad luck: 'I've never tasted anything like it since. It must have been dumped on the unsuspecting English by the French.'

The upside of this disturbing experience was that they started with a clean slate. They weren't copying. Claire, following her husband's example, went back to school to study hard and soft cheesemaking at Sparsholt. It's a measure of the difficulties facing beginners, be they ever so talented, that it took this pair of academics six months experimenting to develop a fresh cheese that had a texture they themselves liked, that didn't dry out and that they believed others, who like themselves had no reference point as to how goats' cheese should taste, would enjoy.

Although it doesn't seem such a great number measured against dairy cattle, over 90,000 goats are being milked in England, a figure that grows every year. Three-quarters of what they yield is directed towards cheesemaking. When Chris and Claire took their first Rosary to market, there were probably less than a thousand being exploited commercially. Goats were mobile middle-class garden ornaments for *The Archers* addicts.

If cheesemakers like Mary Holbrook, Lady Angus and Annette Lee wanted milk, they had no choice. They were bound to rely on their own goats. What happened to these pioneers is that their cheesemaking grew so popular that they couldn't cope with both the herd and the cheese. But by the mid-1990s there were larger commercial herds to supply them. Most, with the exception of Mary Holbrook, sold their goats.

Clockwise from above: The creamy white curd is forced through a tube, sliced with a cheese wire, and rolled in herbs or peppercorns.

Chris and Claire found themselves caught in this double-bind. They couldn't expand their herd on their smallholding, so they were buying in surplus that they collected from Oxfordshire. Having watched 600 goats being milked in the time it took them to deal with their own herd of fifty, they knew that theirs had reached the end of the line. For them it was a bigger rift than the loss of a few pigs, not least because their young children liked the animals.

The Rosary dairy has the look, and something resembling the smell, of an operating theatre. It's designed to minimise any chance of unwanted bacteria entering the food chain. The milk is piped directly into a tank where it's pasteurised slowly at a low temperature (forty minutes at 18°C/65°F). The starter is added, then, after a short delay, the rennet. Once the curd is ready, it's flushed from the tank into a long trough where the whey is allowed to drain. It's salted, shaped and wrapped in clingfilm.

Having stuck to the same process for almost twenty years, they have developed a familiarity

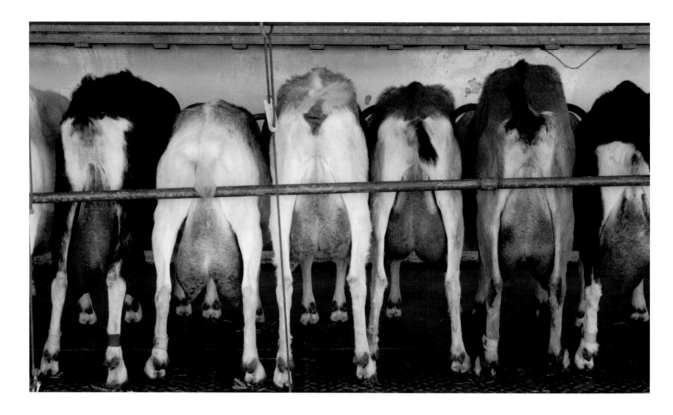

with it that allows them to speak with authority on what happens if they deviate from the standard; for instance the changes that occur when the milk isn't pasteurised. Chris believes that raw milk doesn't noticeably alter the taste, but it does the texture. It produces a somewhat softer curd, making for a smoother mouth-feel.

He can afford to make the concession because he's aware that Rosary is up there with the best fresh cheeses. It has a sprightly lemony taste, which mellows a little when it reaches two to three weeks. The pepper-and-ash coated versions or a Rosary dosed with garlic and parsley, may owe their ancestry to papa Boursin, but they would never be confused with the branded product.

Although they succeeded long ago in their joint ambition to quit the laboratory and the nine-to-five routine, they haven't quite dug up their scientific roots. Chris is fascinated by geotrichum, 'It grows like a weed', that may or may not be a yeast or a fungus. Like *Penicillium candidum* it plays a critical

Goats' cheese may come in a bewildering number of shapes and sizes, but it all starts out from the same place.

role in the ripening of some soft and semi-hard cheeses such as St Nectaire. He has made small batches of furry soft cheese that he knows to be delicious, although he dare not risk introducing it in his dairy for fear of what it might do to the Rosary, should it escape from captivity.

The trouble is that against all the odds Chris and Claire have cracked the almost impossible task of producing a fresh, consistent artisan cheese. It isn't something he can afford to jeopardise.

For the present, if he and Claire want to savour what geotrichum can do to cheese, they could do worse than a busman's holiday to France. They went there for the first time in 2005 and, yes, they can tell a Chabichou from a Crottin de Chavignol. They have developed a palate for French goats' cheeses, not all, but those that are as good as their own.

Fresh Goats' Cheese

What is it?

Exactly what it says it is, a cheese that is ready to eat as soon as it has been made. It's distinct from those cheeses that are ripened in some way.

Are all fresh cheeses alike?

There are various styles, made in different ways.

- Lightly salted and moulded, the texture may vary from very fragile to smooth. Occasionally, it may be sold bathing in its whey.
- More mousse-like than the previous, it's often shaped into discs or small logs and can be flavoured with herbs or pepper.
- Fresh goats' cheese can be gently pressed to extract more whey, not so much as would render it dry, but enough to firm up its texture.
- As a spread, more often than not it is sold in tubs.
- Coated fresh cheeses. In France, goats' cheese covered in ash would normally be ripened, but English artisans sometimes sell it fresh.

Are they seasonal?

A goat provides milk nearly all year round, except in the two to three months before kidding – usually in early spring. This means that the supply dips in mid-winter. However, the way goat farming has evolved in England through the creation of large herds means that cheese is available throughout the year.

How should they taste?

No hard and fast rule here, except that there should be no taints or off flavours. Some makers play down the characteristic goat taste, others work with it. Usually, there's a more-or-less pronounced tang that is down to the use of a starter culture when making the cheese. In a way, it's the maker's signature because he or she can control the level, in the same way that saltiness is a matter for individual preference.

How old are they?

This depends on the distribution channels, but they may be as little as two or three days old and anything up to a month.

How should it be stored?

It's intended for immediate consumption, but will keep in a fridge for a week or longer, even if it's at the end of its shelf life, provided it is well wrapped in film to prevent drying out. In any case it won't go off. It should never be frozen, because it's texture would be damaged by ice crystals forming in the curd.

Portioning?

How much depends on appetite. How a cheese is cut is important, especially if only a part of it is being eaten at a sitting. Neat wedges are the best solution with disc or truncated pyramid cheese; logs should be sliced.

Pasteurised v. unpasteurised?

Purists, those who associate goats' cheese with tradition, tend to talk about complexities of flavour. This is true of all the ripened farmhouse cheeses, especially those that emanate from French regions where diet and climate have a bearing. This doesn't really apply to Britain. Providing that pasteurisation is done without affecting the milk's taste, it doesn't reduce the quality of fresh cheese.

Diet?

It's a mixed picture, because the fat levels in both cows' and goats' milk varies. As a rule of thumb it's better to assume that the level of calories, fat and cholesterol are more or less equivalent for both breeds. Bearing in mind that fresh cheese has a higher moisture content than other cheeses, it's fair to assume that a 30g portion, containing up to 10g of fat will weigh in at about 100 calories, with between 17mg and 30mg of cholesterol.

Vinny

Dorset Blue Vinny enjoys a mythical status, partly because nobody knows where it came from, partly because, to all intents and purposes, it died out and was resurrected, and partly because references to it are so sketchy, so oblique by comparison with the historical evidence of Stilton's origins that people tend to fill the gaps by using their imagination.

If it came from anywhere, the most likely area is Blackmore Vale whose heart lies between the River Stour meandering south from Sturminster Newton, through Blandford Forum and the sea near Bournemouth and the main Sherborne – Dorchester road.

In his Wessex novels, Thomas Hardy invented a name for it: the Vale of Little Dairies, contrasting it with Froom Valley, the Valley of Great Dairies, which was the principal cheddar-making region of Somerset during the nineteenth century. Hardy, however, never mentions vinny, though he gives a vivid account of cheesemaking in *Tess of the D'Urbervilles*, whose eponymous heroine is a dairymaid. If one is searching for a poetic endorsement, William Barnes the Dorset poet, who wrote pastorals in dialect, mentions it – once. In a poem about haymaking that is a kind of dialogue between two labourers over lunch ('Nunchen Time'), one complains, 'It would make the busy little chap/Look rather glum, to see his lap/With all his meal of one dry crust/And vinny cheese as dry as dust.' (see feature overleaf). The 'vinny', incidentally, doesn't mean veined as most people would assume, but 'mouldy', which may explain why the yokel doesn't fancy his meal.

Mike Davies made cheeses when he was a student at Cannington Agricultural College near Bridgwater, not Blues, but Cheddar, Caerphilly,

Opposite: Vinny comes from the heart of Hardy Country.
Right: Mike Davies studied cheesemaking as an agricultural student.
Below: Vinny has a different pattern of veining from Stilton.

Hay-meaken. Nunchen Time (extract)

by William Barnes

Our Company would suit en best,
When we do teake our bit o' rest,
At nunch, a-gather'd here below
The sheade thease wide-bough'd woak do drow,
Where hissen froth mid rise, an' float
In horns o' eale, to wet his droat.
J.
Aye, if his swellen han' could drag

A meat-slice vrom his dinner bag.
'T'ud meake the busy little chap
Look rather glum, to zee his lap
Wi' all his meal ov woone dry crowst,
An' vinny cheese so dry as dowst.
A.
Well, I dont grumble at my food, 'Tis
wholesome, John, an' zoo 'tis good.

Wensleydale and Gloucester. This was not because he had a precocious interest in it, but because sixteen girls were taking the course and only one other 'chap'. He had no inkling that the lectures

The cheese is spiked all over to help the blueing.

would be useful. He was going to be a cowman and that is what he became, taking on the tenancy of Woodbridge Farm at Bishop's Caundle with no ambitions beyond milking his herd of Friesians.

That was until the early 1980s when the government imposed the quotas on dairy farmers. Realising that he was about to be left with a surplus which nobody would buy, that his farm would become uneconomical, he considered making cheese but almost immediately rejected the idea on the grounds that there was already enough perfectly good cheddar being made and, in any case, the farmhouse cheddars were themselves going through a lean patch with farmers abandoning cheesemaking.

As a result of a chance conversation, assisted by some lateral thinking, he hit upon Dorset Blue as a possible alternative. None was being produced, but it still existed as a folk memory. A fraudulent version was even being sold to unknown tourists in and around Cerne Abbas where an astute (unscrupulous) farmer was taking deliveries of second-grade Stilton and passing it off as the mythical vinny. Its reputation began to spread and a BBC current affairs programme, taken in by the scam, sent a film crew to locate it, in vain, because it didn't exist.

What the real thing was and how to make it

To Make Cheeses that the Coats may be Pulled of
From an eighteenth-century manuscript

Take seven quarts of the strokings as they come from the cow put into it a quart of Cream, in the heat of Summer let the Cream be cold, but as the weather grows cold put it in Scalding hot, but heat not the Milke; put therin a good spoonful of Rennet, then stirre it well together, cover it & let it stand till the Curd comes, then with a Dish lay the Curd as whole as you can in a Cloth in the Vate, and when you [have] filled the Vate put the Cloth together & lay the Flower on it, & let it stand for half an houre, then lay the Cloth smooth, & put 18 pound weight on it, & let it stand 4 hours unstirred, then turne it upon the Flower & Salt it then turne it into a clean Cloth into the Vate again, and lay so much and half so much more weight upon it, & let it stand till more Whey com out. Then turn it into a clean drye Cloth; let it remain no mare in the Vate, but lye in a Cloth on the Floore, & as the Cloth wets, turn it to drye, & when it don wetting the Cloth, put it into Rushes, & cover it with rushes, & turn it Twice a day. If the weather [be] hote, cover it not; if the weather be cold cover it with a woolen Cloth. It will be ready in 10 days to eate.

hadn't been quite lost. It was preserved in a Ministry of Agriculture pamphlet. The key difference between vinny and Stilton was that it was made with skimmed milk for the very good reason that Dorset dairies were renowned for their butter. Milk from the previous evening settled overnight, the cream was ladled off and any spare milk went for cheese. Why it had vanished remains a mystery. It could have been a casualty of the Second World War when all but hard cheeses were banned. More likely, it disappeared because it had no commercial value. Farms would produce a little for their own consumption in the same way that they made cider for the labourers.

The 'blueing' was universally considered to be desirable since it improved the taste of what might otherwise have been a dry, flat and uninteresting cheese, especially when set alongside the Somerset cheeses. Initiating the blue veining was the hard part. The dodges used – some of which have passed into legend – seem to have ranged from hit and miss to downright toxic. Shire-horse harnesses were trailed through the milk. Cheeses were laid on damp floors or in the fore bays of the old cow stalls, on hessian sacks or next to old boots. Mouldy breadcrumbs were stirred into the curd. The green ends of copper wires were poked into the cheeses. The most successful solution was probably making the cheeses crack in an already mouldy store.

Mike's initial experiments in his kitchen put an understandable strain on his marriage. Adding *Penicillium roquefortii* increased the chances of his prototype truckles acquiring some sort of blue veining. By storing them in the family pantry he found that salt, sugar, cornflakes changed colour, too.

Growing in confidence, he bought second-hand equipment, converted some outbuildings into a dairy and cheese store and went into production with mixed results.

The ideal vinny, a little smaller than Stilton, has a rough outer rind. When it's cut open, the veining, more flecked than in other blues, should cover the surface with a fine tracery. There should be little or

no browning from the rind into the cheese itself. If there is, it doesn't affect the taste, but it can be off-putting. The texture, given that most of the cream has been skimmed, is less friable than might be expected. Fully ripe, it may not have the unctuousness of Stilton, but it has plenty of body. Its taste is tangy rather than sharp.

Before he succeeded in achieving a modest level of consistency, Mike had to endure the frustration of trying to follow a set procedure and finding that in spite of his best endeavours things were going wrong. Not all his cheeses blued: if they did, then not in the right place. Cracked rinds were a recurring headache for him. His vinny often finished up slipcoated. In the eighteenth century 'Slipcoat' was a desirable kind of cheese in its own right, distinguished by the fact that its rind peeled off. For Mike it was a nuisance.

On one occasion he lost a whole batch because his cows had been binging on turnips. The resultant cheese was so fatty that it collapsed when it was emptied from the moulds. Like so many of his peers, he wrote off dozens if not hundreds of failed cheeses. To add to his difficulties he had to cope with an obtuse Environmental Health Officer, who wanted him to wash down the walls of his store not realising that the moulds developing there were essential to the blueing process.

With hindsight, he would say that the early years were 'interesting and exciting', but also very stressful: 'Several times I could willingly have given up. It's just that I saw that milking cows alone wouldn't do and that I would have to struggle on.'

Perhaps Mike should re-christen his cheese 'New Blue Vinny', because he has refined his technique, using tricks that would not have been open to farmers a century ago. He still skims his morning milk in exactly the same way, but mixes milk powder

These pages: Ideally the blueing should be dispersed evenly through the cheese, from the rind to the centre.

into it to raise the fat level. After adding the starter, rennet and inoculating it with *Penicillium*, it's cut four times, stirred and left in the vat overnight for the curd to settle before the whey is drawn off. The curd is re-cut into blocks, hand-milled, salted and pressed in the moulds by hand, before being put aside for five days with daily turning.

For the first twenty years, Priscilla, his cheesemaker, had to spike each cheese with a skewer one hundred times to assist the blueing. Nowadays there is a contraption similar to the ones that Stilton makers have which does the job in eight seconds. Mike's store, dark, low-ceilinged, musty, faintly sinister, is packed with row upon row of cheeses. Most are neat cylinders gathering crusts, but not all. There are a few smaller ones, a lop-sided one and an occasional split one. It's evidence that this isn't some safe, standardised product. Every morning, as a part of his routine, Mike comes here to grade. Nothing escapes his scrutiny.

It took him four years to obtain a Protected Geographical Indication (PGI) certification for Dorset Blue Vinny from the EU whose officials had to be satisfied that no identical cheese was being produced in Galicia, Piedmont, Luxembourg or any other corner of Europe. Soon after he had obtained it, he received a visit from an official who wanted to charge him a four figure sum for a twice yearly check – 'Only a few cents per cheese' – to ensure that Mike was making it the way he had said he was. Mike sent him on his way and contacted a local Weights and Measures man who checks for free.

In theory, this recognition allows anyone else wanting to start 'vinnying' within the county to do so. It might encourage others to attempt making this capricious cheese. In practice, Mike doesn't feel threatened because a potential rival would have to follow his method in detail and, it's not something he is going to share. A defensible commercial stance, it does mean that the cheese risks a second extinction should he decide to pack up. He's fortunate in that he has already set about ensuring his succession. His son Richard has taken over the farm. Daughter Emily was being groomed to replace him in the dairy, but while his plans for her haven't exactly backfired, they have been given an unexpected twist.

Emily returned from farmers' markets in Sherborne and Dorchester where she had been selling cheese for her father with the idea of converting the leftovers and off-cuts to soup. Until then, he had been content to send these and any unsaleable cheese to a powder manufacture, who processed them and moved them on for coating snack foods such as crisps. Her suggestion developed into the Dorset Blue Soup Company that she runs at

These pages: Mike's son has taken charge of the dairy farming and his daughter has built up a successful cottage industry selling blue cheese soups.

the opposite end of the farmyard from the dairy.

These have had an instant success because they contain no additives, taste good and the cheese dose is so small, barely more than a seasoning, that it doesn't overpower the other fresh ingredients in the soup. Accidentally, Emily is exploiting an aspect of cheese that has been overlooked. It contains free glutamic acid – as in monosodium glutamate – that enhances flavour. Different kinds contain varying amounts, but Parmesan, for instance has significant levels of it.

It's a fact often conveniently forgotten because of the food polemics surrounding MSG, that the Japanese professor, Kikunae Ikeda, credited with

identifying *umami*, was studying food in a Western diet when he discovered that, 'There is a taste which is common to asparagus, tomatoes, cheese and meat but which is not one of the four well-known tastes of sweet, sour, bitter and salty.' It is the industrial overkill with synthesised glutamate that threatens health, not the naturally occurring amino acid, one of the building blocks of protein.

Having made vinny for half his working life, Mike Davies is in a unique position. He can say with confidence that nobody in Dorset knows, or has ever known, as much about it as he does. Nobody has made as much as he has. Probably nobody has made it as well as he has. If his had tasted 'as dry as dust', he would never have been able to sell it. Only once has he met anyone else with a personal memory of it being made, a farming colleague who recalled his mother making some. More often than not it never blued.

In the Giant's Shadow

Visitors to Cerne Abbas, and there are plenty, go there for the mild frisson of viewing the giant whose outline cut into the steep hillside dominates the Dorset village. In his right hand he holds a 120-foot gnarled club, but what attracts the crowds is his smaller though no less impressive tackle. Is he prehistoric, Roman, Saxon, or a

relative late-comer carved out of the turf in the seventeenth century when the earliest written references to him are found?

Because he's the main and only attraction, all the traffic gravitates towards him. Few if any trippers bother with the side lanes that vanish between the hedgerows into beautiful lost combes. One such

combe winds its way over Hog's Hill, Cowdown, across a ford, then another, and turns right to the hamlet of Up Sydling. There's an organic farm shop here and behind it is a white door leading to the domain of Woolsery Cheese.

Opposite: Cerne Abbas provides a dramatic backdrop for Woolsery cheese.
Above: Annette Lee moved her dairy from Woolsery in Devon, where she learned her craft, to Dorset.

Ravioli of Goats' Cheese, Basil and Spinach, with a Rosemary Cream Sauce

Michael Caines built his reputation as the head chef at Gidleigh Park on the edge of Dartmoor, in the mid-1990s. He is now the moving force behind a growing number of luxury hotel-restaurants that bear his name, including one in his home-town of Exeter where he always has a specialist cheese menu.

Serves 8

1 egg and three yolks
20g basil purée
pinch of salt
20ml basil oil
250g plain flour
320g mould-ripened goats' cheese (e.g. ripe Capricorn)
10 chopped basil leaves
salt and pepper
400g young spinach

For the rosemary cream sauce:
200ml whipping cream
1 fresh sprig rosemary

For the picked mixed salad:
Selection of fresh chervil, parsley, tarragon and chives
Olive oil
Lemon juice
100g red peppers, finely diced
100g tomatoes, finely diced

Blend the egg and yolks, purée, pinch of salt and oil in a food processor. Add the flour and blend again. Add a scant tablespoon of water and blend to a supple dough. Blend the cheese, chopped basil, salt and pepper until it's almost smooth.

Roll out the dough on a pasta machine as finely as it will go. Cut out forty circles with a large (3–4 inch) pastry cutter. Put a little of the cheese mixture on each raviolo, fold it in half and crimp the edges. Cook for six minutes in boiling, salted water, drain and cool.

Blanch the spinach in salted water, drain, squeeze out the excess liquid and form forty small nuggets.

For the rosemary cream sauce, bring the whipping cream to a simmer and infuse the rosemary for four minutes. Remove, season the cream and froth it up with a hand blender.

For the salad, mix the herbs with a little olive oil and lemon juice to taste and season with salt. Stew the red peppers in a tablespoon of olive oil and when it's soft add the tomato.

To finish, put a small pile of herb salad in the centre of each plate. Arrange the ravioli around it, each one sitting on spinach. Coat with the rosemary sauce. Dot the tomato-pepper mix in the gaps.

Woolsery is a hard, aged cheese with a clean but light goaty taste.

The name has nothing to do with sheep, nor anything to do with Dorsetshire. It comes from Devon, a contraction of an older form, Woolfardisworthy – 'Wulfheard's wood'– which leads to more confusion because two villages, a few miles apart, are called this. To further complicate matters, Annette Lee the cheesemaker used to be Annette Lee the goat farmer.

A city girl with a love of animals, a sketchy knowledge of animal husbandry and a marriage to an airline pilot behind her, she decided in 1990 that goats were going to be her thing, after listening to a radio programme. She took advice where she could find it. She advertised. She travelled the country collecting livestock in the back of a hired transit van. She built up a herd, which she milked by hand. She expanded it, acquiring goats from a cheesemaker, Graham Townsend, with a growing reputation for his Vulscombe, then sold the milk back to him. Finally, she woke up to the precariousness of her situation when a client cancelled an order leaving her with a surplus that finished up as a pigs'

These pages: The landscape looks idyllic but the peace was shattered by a foot-and-mouth epidemic.

breakfast, but might as well have been poured down the drain.

If, she thought, her customers were converting her milk to cheese, why couldn't she? A smallholder's course at Bicton College for which she had enrolled was cancelled, but undaunted she traced the teacher scheduled to take it, explained that she was in a hurry to learn cheesemaking and asked for help. Rita Ash, who turned up at the farm with a do-it-yourself kit, was a retired tutor from an agricultural college. She had also been an international consultant on cheesemaking, working in Jordan, Tanzania, Zambia and India, as well as for the Ministry of Agriculture.

Annette explained she wanted to make something that would keep so that it wouldn't be wasted if it wasn't sold immediately. Rita demonstrated a recipe similar to Cheshire and watched her pupil try it out before leaving with a promise to return when their cheeses had ripened.

Between visits, Annette practised making one at a time, so that when Rita showed up again, she had prepared several samples. The teacher's verdict was more than encouraging: 'We tasted the cheese she had made and she said it was OK. Then she tasted mine and said: "Oh, that's better." After she had tried the rest, she told me she thought I'd got the knack.'

Analysing what that might be is impossible, but a significant component is patience. For instance, when the nannies are kidding (producing offspring, not inventing misleading stories) the milk is richer and it takes much longer for the whey to drain off the curd. 'It takes how long it takes', is how Annette approaches her daily routine.

At the outset, her only handicap was that she had never liked eating goats' cheese, because what

she had tried reminded her of the animals' smell. 'I don't want my cheese to taste of goat', she told Rita. The answer, she was informed, was to keep the milk as fresh as possible. Encouraged by the fact that she had sold all her prototypes to a Crediton delicatessen, she was determined to keep going. She converted a small outbuilding, outfaced planners, fought obstructive, nit-picking Environmental Health Officers who tried every trick

Opposite: A Woolsery experiment – 'smoked goats' cheese'.

they knew to put her off and turned professional.

In 1999, she had started selling part of her herd to concentrate on the cheese when Rita Ash, now a close friend, contacted her. Would she consider moving from Devon to Dorset, where the manager of a 3,000-acre estate who was forming his own large herd of goats, could put premises and all the extra milk she needed at her disposal? She would advise the farmer with stocking and help him bring the milk's quality to the level she wanted, but would continue making her own cheese.

At Woolfardisworthy, she had been living at the end of a beaten track. Carriers had refused to collect from her. She had found herself fixing meetings in car parks where truckles would surreptitiously change hands. Her dairy unit was too small. The local EHO was on her back to fit a ventilation unit. By moving away she may have been uprooting herself, but the roots didn't go down deep.

Having bedded herself down in a well-equipped dairy and her remaining goats a few miles away, she was growing accustomed to a more settled regime when the foot-and-mouth epidemic of 2001 struck. The outbreak would lead to the destruction of two-and-a-half million farm animals in the affected counties. Television screens filled nightly with images of burning sheep and cattle carcases. It was government policy to slaughter all animals in any area where an outbreak had occurred regardless of whether they were sick or not. It succeeded in keeping the disease out of Dorset, where Annette was making her Woolsery. By sheer bad luck, though, her goats were kept on land across the Dorset border in Somerset, ten miles away. When the herd was condemned she had no means of saving them: 'It was tragic. I felt cut off because I couldn't go to the farm where they were and I couldn't come to the dairy. We couldn't communicate except on the telephone. The local vets went through a terrible time during the first few days because they said we were perfectly OK, but they were overruled by London that said the goats had to be put down. The army came and I'm really glad I didn't see it because they were put down and carried away in skips.'

With no milk of her own, Annette, once she could begin cheesemaking again, relied on the estate's goats that had been safely stabled on the 'safe' side of the county border. This lasted two more years until the property was sold. The new owner had no plans to carry on farming goats and sold them all.

When, at the outset, she had collected her stock in the back of the van, milk was scarce, large herds few and far between. In a decade, goat farming had become fashionable enough for her to find new sources to bail her out.

Across the Channel, anyone committed to producing *fromage de chèvre* focuses on the difference in flavour between goats' and cows' milk. There are famous restaurants such as Troisgros at Roanne that present their fresh goats' cheeses on a separate cheeseboard so that connoisseurs may choose according to their taste, a drier, moister, younger, older, harder, softer one: one that may come from a peasant smallholding where a handful of goats have grazed on wild thyme and savory or one from a pedigree commercial herd. At both ends of the range a 'goaty' taste is essential because, over centuries people have acquired a liking for it.

In England, where no similar tradition exists, that characteristic tang can shock the palate. Not liking it herself has been a boon to Annette who has only ever made cheeses she can eat and enjoy. Her taste is in tune with the public's. Even her four-month-old hard cheese, that has plenty of acidity and a long lingering taste, doesn't have an up-front, in-your-face 'goatiness'. It's there, of course, but balanced out, rather than aggressively present.

When she described it as her 'bread and butter', she probably meant that it kept her bank manager happy, but it is the kind of everyday all-year-round cheese that doesn't cloy. Woolsery isn't her only cheese, she does fresh cheeses for the markets and delis – so fresh and moist that they may go fizzy if they aren't eaten at once.

It could be mischievous to suggest that all cheeses reflect their creators, but some do: Joe Schneider's Daylesford echoes a meticulous, academic temperament; Frances Wood's Junus is an original and unpredictable one; Robin Congdon's Beenleigh has an intuitive, biting perception. Annette's appear to be understated and yet they are gritty and full of substance. Her Fiesta, may have begun as an attempt at feta (Rita Ash again came to her aid by supplying a recipe), but it has its own distinct personality.

European law now protects the name and origin of feta, insisting that it must be manufactured in Greece if it's to carry the name. Generally made from sheep's or sometimes goats' milk to form a hard, crumbly curd that's soaked in brine, it's been copied by the German and Danish food industry using cows' milk. When Annette determined on producing a feta-style cheese, she checked out the competition and found it 'revolting'. For once she wasn't objecting to the 'goaty' flavour so much as the heavy salting that dominates both the Greek artisan and the factory versions.

To a shepherd on Naxos or Crete, feta is a bite to take out of one's knapsack along with a crust of barley bread, a meal that hasn't changed during two millennia. Pickled it keeps for a year. Annette's feta-style recipe softens the texture. It crumbles, but doesn't have the rubbery body of the factory-made brands.

In Greece, after soaking in a concentrated solution, feta can absorb between six and eight per cent of its weight in salt. To put this into perspective, Stilton makers are currently being encouraged to lower their current two per cent content, and most cheeses weigh in at about one-and-a-half. On a baking hot Mediterranean mountainside, a chunk of salty cheese may energise a working man. In cooler latitude, however, it doesn't fit, whereas Fiesta that's been marinated in a light whey brine, goes down a treat with a salad of tomatoes, olives, basil and a coating of Greek oil.

Because she has had to struggle against adversity, being her own boss, working unassisted until she came to Up Sydling, Annette has developed a kind of freelancer's approach to selling her cheeses. They are on the shelves of Sainsbury's and Waitrose, but also at a dozen farmers' markets where she'll also sell a cheddar she's made for the curious who stop by, sniff and say that they don't buy goats' cheese. She deals with about forty delis and key wholesalers, attends shows such as the nearby Sturminster Newton Cheese Festival set up as an in memoriam to the co-operative dairy that Dairy Crest closed down in 2000. It's a 'Don't put all your eggs in one basket' approach that she hopes will cushion her against the innate weaknesses of any newcomer in a volatile niche market.

For much of the time she has been a single mother raising a son who would have nothing to do with goats. That, she hopes, is changing: 'Now he can see what we've done he might get involved.'

Whenever she refers to the difficulties she has encountered, she repeats the sentence, probably unconsciously: 'I wouldn't be beaten.' It is a very appropriate motto for a strong lady with more balls than the giant on the hill.

Opposite: Triumph over tribulation. Having overcome the loss of her herd, Annette can once again afford to smile.

The Road to Cranborne Chase

'Ashmore' is emblematic of the random way in which most modern British cheeses have come into being. It began as a recipe designed for smallholders published in a textbook by the North of Scotland College of Agriculture and has ended up on Lord Salisbury's estate at Cranborne Chase, having undergone enough twists and turns to fill a Trollope novel, Anthony or Joanna.

Twenty-something years ago, David Doble, a Sussex dairy farmer, thought he would have to start making cheese when he woke up to the fact that he had ninety cows and a quota for sixty. Also a beekeeper, he outlined his intentions with a fellow

enthusiast who owned a copy of the Scottish book and was making cheese as a hobby. She invited him to watch her. He accepted, observed her efforts with a saucepan and the kitchen range and decided that the process couldn't be much harder than apiculture and made his first attempt.

He bought himself a length of plastic drainpipe that, sawn up, would be his moulds, and a four-gallon bucket for the milk. He borrowed his daughter's sterilised terry cloth nappies to drain the curd, hanging them from the ceiling in satsuma bags. At three months he had what passed for a cheese.

The next stage involved 'massive' expansion. He

Opposite: Working Victorian cheese presses are a feature of Ashmore dairy.
Above: Wooden rakes are used for stirring the curds.

travelled to Wales to buy a second-hand fifty-gallon vat from a fellow farmer and took one of his cheeses to have it appraised by the vendor. Although it received a polite approval from the Welshman, David gathered that he had not grasped the faintest inkling of what he had let himself in for. He hadn't kept records of his batches. He didn't measure the acidity of the curd. Nor had he realised how vulnerable a farmhouse cheese was to the most minute circumstance.

The lessons were learnt the hard way. He had been maturing cheeses in his spare bedroom on a board placed across the bed. In winter, with the central heating on, the cheeses dried out and cracked. In summer flies managed to get into his making room. They laid their eggs in the curd, filling his cheeses with maggots. He was, though, making progress, winning a prize for the Best New Cheese at the International Food Exhibition (IFE) at Olympia.

For eight years he continued making and selling. Growing more professional, he bought larger vats and increased volume, but unfortunately it coincided with a time when he realised that his farm wasn't making money; that he would have to close down.

At this point, Mrs Vigor, recently widowed, comes on the scene. She was running a neighbouring farm, across the Surrey border, which was larger and more economic. Her grown-up son wanted to join her. Having learnt from her sister, an employee of David's, that he was packing up, she thought she might be able to acquire the

Opposite: David Doble runs his hand through the whey to test the curds.
Right: A domestic kitchen sieve serves to fill the moulds.

redundant cheesemaking equipment, borrow some of David's know-how, and fill the gap in the market that he would be leaving.

Mrs Vigor, later to become Pat Doble, picked up the baton, bought his business and, after some hands-on training from David, converted herself into a cheesemaker. The two of them are convinced that the quality of any cheese is tied to the milk. Pat helped her son to switch from a herd of 120 English cattle to 60 Friesian, bought in Brittany, that supplied the same amount of milk. Her cheeses went to Neal's Yard Dairy. The herd was assessed as one of the country's top ten.

What the French call a *succès d'estime*, a moral triumph, wasn't adding up to a financially secure position. Neither the cheese nor the dairy farm was failing, but Pat's son convinced her that they should quit. By now, Pat and David were living together. After the sale went through, they decided that they would start afresh, doing what they both understood: making cheese.

They moved to Ashmore, a village on the Wiltshire-Dorset border near Shaftsbury, and they married. Their new landlord rented them a dairy. He also supplied them with milk from his herd. The arrangement should have suited both parties, but instead it led to conflict. The landlord wanted to go into a partnership with the Dobles. He felt they should be creative, devise never-done-before cheeses such as 'red Gorgonzola'. They were purists. Even the idea of mixing in chives gives them the shivers. They wanted to retain their independence, so they turned him down.

They had already registered their business name, but soon afterwards they were contacted in an official letter from the National Business Register warning them that someone was applying to

trademark their name, Ashmore Farm Cheese. They put two and two together and concluded that their landlord, who wasn't making any cheese himself, was behind it.

It was time for another move. Ashmore is at the northern edge of Cranborne Chase, the ancient royal hunting ground that, until the nineteenth century, had severe laws to deal with poachers, including execution and mutilation. It's divided up, much of it, into estates belonging to the landed gentry. One of the largest, owned by Lord Salisbury, is centred around Cranborne. Its biggest asset is property, but it runs shoots, and manages woodland and farms.

At a farmers' market, by chance, Pat met Lord

Salisbury's farm manager. She inquired whether he might have any spare buildings into which she could transfer the cheesemaking business. Once there had been three dairies on the estate, but all had shut down. Most of the 4,000 acres under cultivation has been turned over to arable crops. However, Lord Salisbury does have a personal interest in livestock. Shades of P.G. Wodehouse's *Blanding Castle,* he extensively rears breed pigs: large blacks, middle whites and Tamworths. These are sold as meat in the Cranborne food shop owned by the estate. As there was an indirect synergy and since there was a hangar available just outside the village, the Dobles were invited to move in.

No longer made in Ashmore, Ashmore Farm Cheese is now produced on his lordship's land. This is quite confusing since another cheesemaker,

trading as Cranborne Chase Cheese is making three soft cheeses, Filly Loo, St Nicholas and Win Green at Ashmore.

The couple brought with them the equipment that they had collected over twenty years – the original fifty-gallon vat, two other larger ones, the moulds and a motley assortment of mainly antique presses. When David was teaching himself the rudiments, he had relied on two, one-ton concrete blocks to weight his cheeses. These served their purpose in the short term, but weren't an ideal solution in the longer term.

He bought his first proper press for £5. The father of a local vet acquired it for him at a farm sale near Okehampton in Devon. Listed as Lot No. 1, it was damaged and caked in rust, but useable after it was repaired. Actually, it was a snip, because the

Opposite: Young cheeses are pale whereas older ones are dappled with mould.
Below: The freshly made cheeses are on the top racks and the older ones developing moulds are lower down.

cast-iron frame, sandblasted and repainted, will last forever. In fact, in the Victorian era a similar press would have cost £2.10.0. to buy new, more than a month's wages for a farm labourer.

In the Cranborne dairy there are a dozen working antique presses bought from all over England, each one still working. An 1856 advertisement for their 'prizewinning' Rack and Pinion Cheese Press, made by Denings of Chard, boasted: 'Greatly improved by means of a roller being placed on each side of the follower, thereby preventing friction. The pressure can be regulated from 12 to 16 cwt by means of the weight being made to shift on the lever.' The 'follower' in the copy was a circular hardwood disc that fitted between the mould and the press.

Although their tools may be antiquated, the Dobles' dairy would have many of their peers looking on with envy. It's spacious, bright, impeccably clean, with a view onto open fields where rare White Park cattle graze. Cheeses that have been formed in Caerphilly moulds line the store in ordered rows. At four months, when they are ready to eat, they have a firm texture that retains just a hint of moisture. They have a clean lactic smell and just enough acidity to give them an edge.

David describes himself as 'mad about cheese'. What he objected to most when his previous landlord had suggested they should join forces was the latter's readiness to compromise standards, to put commercial expediency before quality. 'We would never,' David insisted, 'think of selling something that wasn't perfect.' His is an old-fashioned craftsman's pride in his skill.

That determination is shared by Pat. In a corner of the store she has been experimenting with a semi-hard cheese that she tried to perfect when she was on her farm. She had made it in a cellar and called it Tillingbourne. Once, when James Aldridge had dropped by, she had brought him one that she had been ripening, illegally had she intended selling it, in a damp cellar. The Beckenham cheesemonger

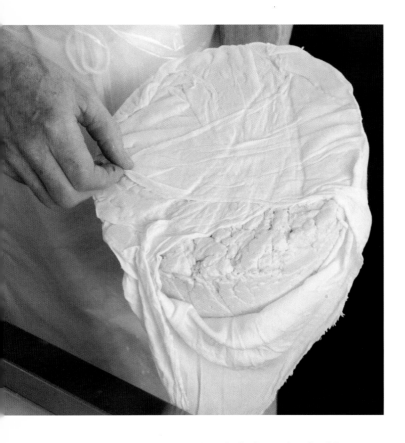

Above: Removing the cloth from the freshly pressed curd.
Opposite: David and Pat Doble, romantically attached by cheese.

had tasted it and beamed: 'I'm really proud of you, Pat. You'll probably never do it again.'

His backhanded praise hasn't prevented her trying, although at Cranborne she fears that her store, regulated for ripening the hard cheese, isn't moist enough for her semi-hard.

Both she and David regret that they no longer own their herd. They have, though, opted for the next best thing by working with a farmer who is ready to share detailed information on what he has been feeding his cows. He'll take their advice not to add certain foodstuffs to the cows' diet, for instance kale, which might cause taint. They have never deviated from raw milk as the basis for Ashmore.

Should they or the public that buys their cheese be frightened of E. coli, listeria or tuberculosis? Listeria has never caused any problems with hard cheese. E. coli, which can cause serious food poisoning, has been spread by contaminated cheese. What is not realised in the general hysteria that is whipped up by the media if a case occurs, is that people are far more likely to suffer an E. coli attack by drinking water from a vending machine or, outside of the UK, by drinking tap water.

As to tuberculosis, the fear of unwittingly making cheese from infected milk has persuaded many specialist cheesemakers to pasteurise. Pat argues that her milk comes from a single herd that is tested monthly. In any event, the disease develops slowly. It isn't present in the milk until the disease is well advanced, by which time it would have been diagnosed in the herd and the cows put down.

When they go to markets the Dobles feel they are encouraging their customers to distance themselves from the mass-produced product in order to develop a sense of respect for crafted food. Once people set their expectations higher, and taste a little more carefully, they will be repaid by the extra pleasure that the unpasteurised cheese offers them. That there is an accelerating change in the way those who can afford to are eating is borne out by Pat and David's experience at Winchester Farmers' Market. In its early days they were the only cheesemaker. Now there are seven.

Step over the threshold of Lord Salisbury's Cranborne Stores and the same commitment to food that has been produced carefully and on a small scale is equally apparent. This isn't a smart deli. Despite its ownership, it's the village shop. Yes, it stocks Brillo pads, Mars Bars, Heinz Ketchup and the *Daily Mail,* but the meat counter is packed with the pork that almost disappeared from English tables during the lean-good-fat-bad decades of intensively farmed cheap meat, and it also has a counter with Ashmore, Woolsery, Keen's, Daisy and a dozen more cheeses.

Thinking Inwardleigh

Brisk, co-ordinated, repeating long-grooved gestures, Rachel Stephens working in her dairy is every bit the expert. Twenty years of making Curworthy hasn't soured her complexion or clouded her blue eyes.

A Wiltshire farmer's daughter, not long out of college, she had moved with her husband and first child to a small Devon farm between Okehampton and Hatherleigh in March 1979. They had been lucky to acquire it so young. She had been contract milking. John had been running a farm near Swindon for a step-uncle who was waiting for developers to buy the land. When he sold up, he split the dairy herd and

equipment down the middle with his nephew.

It was a risk that could have backfired when the galloping inflation that pushed up interest rates stretched their borrowing to the limit. They switched to milking their forty cows three times a day as a means of increasing yield without spending any capital they didn't have. That additional pressure tested John's ability as a stockman to the limit. The cattle may not resent the extra visit to the milking parlour, but they are more at risk from lameness or mastitis.

By now Rachel's children had begun playschool. In a rural community, the school gate is arguably more influential than the local pub for spreading news and networking. There she met another young mother, married to the manager of Curworthy Farm in the nearby village of Inwardleigh, one, she discovered, that was in the public eye: 'Farmers Weekly used to run a farm at Inwardleigh and they used to write about it. They had several, one in the East that was arable, one in France and this one, a dairy farm and one of the bigwigs of the magazine decided they would start cheesemaking with their milk.'

Their recipe, similar to Dutch Gouda, had been supplied by the Agricultural Development and Advisory Service (ADAS), but they were going to present it as a semi-hard seventeenth-century cheese. They employed a young, professional cheesemaker and converted an old stable for making cheese.

Before the grand opening Rachel was approached by the manager's wife, who asked whether she would mind lending a hand: 'They were going to have a launch and they got a local

Left: Devon Oke is made to the same 17th century recipe as Curworthy and matured longer.
Below: Curworthy antique press – like Tess of the d'Urbevilles would have used.

Cheese on Toast

"'Tis time I were choked by a bit of toasted cheese.'

Shakespeare's *Merry Wives of Windsor*

Welsh rabbit or 'rarebit' belongs to a family of toasted cheese that goes back to Saxon times. It's always delicious, always indigestible, regardless of how it's made.

Gentlemen out on the town in Edwardian times used to eat it in the same way that today's roisterers order curry or kebabs.

There is no definitive version, but the American author Robert Carlton Brown came close to nailing the subject in *The Complete Book of Cheese* by giving sixty-five versions!

The trick when stewing cheese is to do it in a double saucepan, or a bowl over a pan of simmering water. Which cheese is best for the job? So long as it's hard, it doesn't matter too much. Mellow or gut-wrenchingly powerful, it's up to the individual to choose.

The basic technique for a rabbit is always the same:

1. Heat the ale in the top pan until it's hot.
2. Add grated cheese and keep stirring.
3. Once it has melted stir until the mixture is creamy and silky (if it hardens or turns stringy that's a failure, but you can still eat the result).
4. Mix in any extra ingredients, such as mustard, pepper or cream.
5. Beat a little more and pour over the hot toast, either buttered or soaked in ale.

MP and the press to launch the cheese and they needed help with teas, cutting up the cheese and they said, "Do you want a job for a couple of hours?" and I thought, "Fair enough, have a look round" and so I did. I went up on launch day and several months later it was beginning to sell and she said: "How would you like a part-time job while the children are at play school?"'

The habit of cheesemaking grew on Rachel: 'You were doing it right from the beginning. One minute, it's milk in the morning and by four in the afternoon it's solid which is fascinating, really.'

By this time the professional cheesemaker had left and there was one other girl working in the dairy. They made various sizes, all with the same recipe. Curworthy, after the farm, was the brand on which the publicity was showered. Belstone, named after another village, was a vegetarian copy. Devon Oke, a larger cheese, was aged six or seven months.

They were successful, too. Smart London stores such as Harrods bought them. Instead of being a paragraph in a trade magazine's diary column, a token nod to the fashionable cry for farmers to diversify, Curworthy Farm had evolved into a lively cottage industry.

Rachel had been working short of three years there when the couple that managed it left. When *Farmers Weekly* set about hiring a replacement, they wanted to separate the cheese business from the rest of the 800-acre farm: 'They decided that, as the cheese business was growing, it was too much for the farm manager to do the cheese as well. They felt he couldn't do justice to both jobs. So they advertised it as a franchise. They wanted someone to go there, use the farm's milk for it, but run the cheese side as their own business, but renting the equipment and the building. But

Devon Oke is a larger, aged version of Curworthy.

they also wanted to continue writing about how you were getting on in their magazine.'

'My husband said, like they do, "That's a good idea. You go and do that and perhaps we can use our own milk eventually." So I applied and I did say we'd like to make it our own business if it proved

worthwhile. We thought we could find out without having to invest much capital.'

They signed a contract that committed Rachel to another three years at Inwardleigh, buying the farm's milk and carrying on as before, except that there was rent to pay and customers to find. The term completed, she and John took up their option to close the Curworthy dairy, buy its equipment including the antique presses and scales she still has and relocate. Helped by a grant, they built their own dairy, free to take their own decisions. It was an uncomplicated decision taken to make a little extra profit from their herd.

Rachel was not intending to reinvent the cheese: 'Curworthy was the original name and we kept it because it had gained its place. The only thing we changed was the milk and to be honest it was better because up there they had a cowman who was employed by them. It made no difference to him how good the milk was. Whereas when you're doing it for yourself, John doing the milking, it's better and better for the cheese. He always felt – well, his father said: "Always treat your cows like a bank. The more you put in, the more you get out."'

However limited her ambitions, Curworthy was improving, changing from a concept aimed at

Passion in the Dairy

From *Tess of the D'Urbervilles* by Thomas Hardy

They were breaking up the masses of curd before putting them into the vats. The operation resembled the act of crumbling bread on a large scale; and amid the immaculate whiteness of the curds Tess Durbeyfield's hands showed themselves of the pinkness of the rose. Angel, who was filling the vats with his handful, suddenly ceased, and laid his hands flat upon hers. Her sleeves were rolled far above the elbow, and bending lower he kissed the inside vein of her soft arm.

Although the early September weather was sultry, her arm, from her dabbling in the curds, was as cold and damp to his mouth as a new-gathered mushroom, and tasted of the whey. But she was such a sheaf of susceptibilities that her pulse was accelerated by the touch, her blood driven to her finer-ends, and the cool arms flushed hot.

Curworthy cheese was first made on a farm managed by the magazine Farmers Weekly.

providing entertainment for magazine readers, into a new product in a sparse market and thence, into one that could stand scrutiny with the best farmhouse cheeses. Rachel credited one of the cheese buyers who called by with two significant shifts away from the *Farmers Weekly* formula.

'When we first worked up there, we used to coat the cheese in something called 'Plasticoat' that was an awful white stuff. It used to smell and I can remember putting it on. Then one of my cheese buyers, a great guy, came down from Somerset, and he had a great sense of cheese and he came in one day and he had a look in my storeroom and he'd come with his iron and he said: "Have you ever thought that instead of using this awful Plasticoat stuff, why don't you coat them with lard?" So that's what we did. It's more natural and it's what we've

done ever since, except for the vegetarian one where we use a solid vegetarian fat.'

His second piece of advice came about by accident. 'There were some of those big cheeses that were sat there and forgotten and the same buyer that told us about the lard, when he saw the big ones, he asked: "What are you doing with them?" and I said: "Nothing at the moment. They are just sitting there." And he went over the moon about Devon Oke and was I making any at the moment? And I thought: "This sounds good", so I started making them again.'

Good decision. It's a kind of Gouda, but in early middle age. It has a thin, biscuit-like rind. Highlighted, the pale-lemon colour would look good in a still life of cheese painted by a seventeenth-century Dutch Master. Firm, rather

The magazine aimed to encourage readers to take an interest in reviving the vanishing craft of cheesemaking.

than medium-hard (classifications tend to confuse: where does medium-hard begin and medium-soft leave off?), it looks as though it ought to be waxy. It isn't except when squeezed between thumb and forefinger. Nor is it crumbly. The smell is clean, light but persistent. 'Buttery' matches the texture it leaves on the tongue and the roof of the mouth, not the taste, which is mature, concentrated without being aggressive. It has a touch of acidity without seeming either sharp or tangy.

It's very good and Rachel has always been proud of it and of protecting its reputation. A supermarket chain wanted to place a large order for a national promotion. She refused, not because she is hostile to the major groups, she isn't, but because she couldn't provide enough fully aged Devonokes to meet the order and wasn't prepared to let them leave her store under-ripe. It's a lesson from which others might benefit.

If that gives the impression of an art-before-income attitude, it shouldn't. She'll happily compromise if it won't affect the standards she's set. The Bath Fine Cheese Company wanted to export Devon Oke to America, but discovered that cheesemongers there preferred the milder, smaller, younger Curworthy. Rachel was happy to allow these to cross the Atlantic where they are sold as 'Devon Oke'.

She also doesn't mind flavouring her hand-crafted cheese with ginger, spring onion or wholegrain mustard. The last of these evolved after Aylesbury Brewery, which had been adding

Curworthy cheese is coated in black, melted wax. First the sides are dipped in it by hand . . .

. . . then the top and bottom, and allowed to set before the labels are added.

beer to pickled onions and mustard asked her to make a cheese with its Chiltern Ale. She took advice, learned that beer could be added to cheese provided that there was no active yeast in it and went ahead. She still makes batches that are sold at the brewery as Chiltern Beer Cheese.

One Christmas she received a jar of wholegrain mustard from the brewery as a gift. For the fun of it, she put some in her beery cheese mixture and 'found that it was lovely'. She's made Meldon ever since.

Her most pragmatic stroke is selling sliced Curworthy, fifteen slices per cheese, to a neighbouring farmer who goes to West Country events, such as point-to-points, selling

cheeseburgers from a trailer.

At Inwardleigh, pasteurisation was the norm because milk was delivered in a mobile tank. She stopped when she moved the cheesemaking to her own farm but has reverted to the original system: 'My Environmental Health Officer told me "If you go down with TB, I'll not allow you to sell your cheese." So we had no choice. We're clear, fingers crossed.' It would take a remarkable palate to notice any difference in the cheeses' taste.

She has also had to cope with another common ailment of farming life, marriage breakdown. She manages the cheese. John still supplies the milk and they own the business jointly. With the shelves of

Below: Rachel Stephens in her store.

her stores packed with neat rows of ripening cheeses, her order books full to bursting and national accounts she can afford to turn down, Rachel could spend her weekdays in the office and weekends with her feet up. It isn't the case. She works twelve-hour shifts in the dairy, hosing down after her girls have returned to their families. At weekends, she has taken to doing a few, select farmers' markets, glad of the human contact she receives by meeting the public who will go back to her and say, 'This is my favourite cheese', rather than professional buyers.

She is one of the *Grandes Dames of speciality* cheesemaking, a master craftsman, respected by her peers.

Roquefort? But not as we know it

Like those ancient monarchs who roamed the countryside followed by an army of courtiers and retainers, Roquefort trails a baggage of myth and history in its wake. About the time William of Normandy was invading England, it received its first written testimonial. By the fifteenth century, the caves in which it matured were protected by royal decree. The philosopher Denis Diderot described it in his eighteenth-century *Encyclopedia* as 'Le Roi des fromages'.

Back in the mists of the 1970s, an English sheep farmer visited the Rocher de Combalou where the famous blues bloom. Impressed by what he saw, he scraped mould spores of *Penicillium roquefortii* from the rock-walls and returned to his Devon domain, determined to switch from the ewes' milk yoghurt he had been making to a 'tribute cheese'.

Thirty years on, Robin Congdon's progress from sheep farmer to cheesemaker has meandered to such a level of craftsmanship that he is internationally recognised for his skill. Beenleigh, his signature blue cheese, is sold around the world. Aspiring artisans from Australia, the USA, Argentina, Italy and Ethiopia have come to work for him. Despite his reputation as a top man, he would readily admit that he has never, ever, made Roquefort.

A signed-up member of the alternative society, the young farmer must have had mixed feelings about the clients for his yoghurt when he drove up to London and parked his Citroën 2CV saloon with the passenger seats removed outside Harrods: 'They gave us the labels, ingredients and price lists, so we'd dash in, try and find a space for the yoghurts on the self-service shelves, and more

Opposite: The switchback hills of the South Hams have proved magnetic to New Age farmers and craftsmen.
Right:. Robin Congdon is a uniquely talented, intuitive cheesemaker.

often the next guy to come along would push all yours to the back and put his in front of them.'

By contrast with the regular toing and froing, the thought of switching to a cheese that would take about five months to ripen seemed less stressful. Sarie Cooper, his partner, had sat in on an ABC of cheesemaking, run as part of a course on smallholding activities, set up by the Dartington Hall Trust, the centre for ecology and the arts founded by the American heiress Dorothy Elmhirst and her husband Leonard. Apart from that, neither of them had any notion of what they were setting out to do. Stilton was the only 'blue' being made in Britain, and apart from Dorset Blue Vinny that had basically become extinct, the only veined cheese with a tradition.

There are no suitable rocky outcrops in the South Hams with ready-made caves where a young couple might leave a few loaves (the French refer to their whole Roqueforts as 'pains') to go mouldy. So Robin decided that he would make one. In the hamlet of Beenleigh near Totnes he acquired a large lump of ground, about the size a Bronze Age warrior might select for his burial mound. Next he bought second hand a wine tank large enough to stand upright in. Stage three, he rented a digger and scooped out a hole into which, step four, he implanted his tank.

If he discovered he had a talent for making cheese, Robin also learned that it didn't turn blue to order. It did and then it didn't, defying logic. Was it the pasture, the milk or the ewes themselves that produced a more compact texture than the crumbly but creamy texture for which he was striving? Hit and miss it certainly was: a journalist who claimed to enjoy this Mk I Beenleigh wrote that it tasted of soap.

Maybe Robin was mulling over ways of improving consistency when he accidentally padlocked Sarie inside the cave. It was her job to turn the Beenleighs over on the shelves as a regular part of the ripening process. Unable to leave, she waited hours underground in a cramped, very smelly store teeming with mites and fungus until Robin, who had gone back to the farm, realised what he had done and returned to release her.

The suggestion of absent-mindedness gives no hint at the single-mindedness that Robin showed in turning himself into a creative, intuitive cheesemaker, giving up his duties as shepherd and milkmaid in the process. 'I suppose I've realised that I'm better at making cheese than farming', he confessed.

Along the way, Beenleigh has not just become reliably veined: it has developed into a unique ewes' milk cheese, still varying, through the year, season on season, but with slight fluctuations that enhance its personality. It's heavier than it once was, perhaps a tad harder, too.

Ironically, now that it is better than it has ever been, Robin prefers another cheese he has invented, Harbourne. Made with goats' milk, it's white speckled with blue veins, quite crumbly,

> **After the fall of the Roman Empire ... the monks of the Benedictine and Cistercian monasteries, thanks to whom the population did not starve to death entirely during the Dark Ages, were the pioneers of the new cheese-making industry of medieval times. If the chronicles of Eginhard, Charlemagne's biographer, are to be believed, it was in one of these monasteries – probably the abbey of Vabres near Roquefort – that the Emperor, another lover of cheese, was given a sheep's milk cheese veined with mould. Much to his surprise, he liked it. He made the prior promise to send two crates of this cheese a year to Aix-la-Chapelle, thus nearly ruining the poor community.**
>
> **From the *History of Food* by Maguelonne Toussaint-Samat, 1987**

almost crunchy when bitten. More piquant than Beenleigh, it has a clean fresh taste that lasts in the mouth. It's closer in style to Roquefort, except that no French *maître fromager* would conceive of choosing goats' milk for a *bleu*.

On paper, the recipes for both might seem indistinguishable – for all three, if you count a cows' milk, Devon Blue – but details that appear insignificant to an outsider can have a dramatic impact, especially on texture. Nick Trant, who has worked with Robin for eight years, has developed the second sense that's necessary to second-guess the invisible alchemy that's going on.

Beenleigh and Harbourne, Nick explained, are stirred and cut differently, but by looking at the vat, he will know whether to cut a little more, stir a little less, leave things an extra minute or so. According to Robin, every cheesemaker has tricks to help him reach the same result that is the key to consistency. His personal fad involves controlling the temperature to a degree. Another's, he suggests, might be about time or the level of acidity.

A researcher from a television company visited the dairy to weigh it up as a potential location for a food feature. He went away and the programme wasn't made, because the dairy 'wasn't picturesque enough'. What the researcher missed was the grace and speed with which Nick works during the critical few minutes when he gathers the curd after it's been drained. It's a kind of muscular ballet, piling curds into polyethylene moulds, then flipping them so the fresh cheese stands proud above the mould like a risen soufflé. Left to settle, it will sink below the rim without losing the open texture that allows the tracery of veining to form during ripening.

Robin's 'cave' has long been abandoned to meet the stringent food safety standards that are in force. Nick wonders what Environmental Health Officers, who police British cheese manufacturers, would make of some continental artisans. He was taken to see an Italian family making Gorgonzola in Lombardy: 'The man who was stirring the vat had a cigarette in one hand. His wife was standing around and there were two cats in the dairy.' That didn't stop them, he added, from producing excellent cheese.

The contrast between the typical *produzione artigianale* and Robin's approach to his craft goes to the heart of what is unique about the modern British cheesemaker. He didn't come from solid peasant stock that had lived for generations on the land, following the same routines, for the same reasons, with the same results because that was what the parents and grandparents had done. He had a choice. He had a degree. He was working for Westminster Bank before he moved to sheep farming. Sarie had been a nurse. Whatever their motives, however idealistic they may have been at the outset, they couldn't pretend they had ties to a

This page: Chef, turned baker, turned cheesemaker, Nick Trant, has become Robin Congdon's invaluable aid.

rural way of life that had already petered out in England because it was uneconomic.

That they've survived, even prospered, has less to do with business plans than an ability to accept changes and turn them to advantage. When the flock was sold, they bought the land at Ticklemore, a hamlet in the parish of Ashprington, near the River Dart that they had been renting for milking and penning the sheep. It allowed Robin to build himself a dairy, not a state-of-the-art gleaming stainless steel temple, more a functional space with minimal technology. If it gets too dry in the ripening rooms, his solution is to empty a bucket of water on the stone floor.

Now that he needed to buy in his milk, he had to heat-treat it, but he managed the shift, which also involved a change of principles, without losing the respect of his peers or harming the

reputation of his wares. Able to focus on the making, he experimented with Ticorino, a pecorino in all but name, creating the young semi-hard Ticklemore Goat, which he now farms out to Debbie Mumford at Sharpham (see p.153). 'They make it better than me', he admitted – probably because his own dairy is impregnated with moulds and spores from his blues, and recently Buttons, a fresh goats' cheese that's named after his Cornish supplier.

He also built himself a house adjoining the dairy: 'There was no planning permission, so we could probably have faced prosecution.' That would have been harsh because, even today it's part office, part staff canteen, dedicated to cheesemaking.

Sarie recognised its impact on their lives: 'You may start off thinking that by doing this you can take charge of your own destiny, but you find that the business drives you.' It's a wry comment from someone who has grasped the chasm between youthful illusions and adult experience.

No longer working in the dairy, Sarie has

opened a cheese shop in Totnes. Neat, bright, welcoming, it's quite unlike the vaguely forbidding sign in the lane outside their Ticklemore Farm announcing: 'No Visitors', which is more a plea for personal privacy, than a thumbs down to the naturally curious. There is no exuberant display of all the cheeses of worth produced within a 100-mile radius, as at Gary and Elise Jungheim's Tavistock shrine (see opposite page). The smell doesn't knock you back: what's on the counter is always laid out discreetly.

That the trippers who poke their noses around the door of the shop should never have heard of Beenleigh is no surprise to her, but she's aggrieved that people who have been living on her doorstep for years walk in, buy a slice of Sharpham, pay and walk out: 'They don't give a toss that *we* make cheese.' The word should have got around. Rationally, she'd admit that her expectations were naïve. Even in Ashprington (population 477 at the last count) villagers don't know who Robin and Sarie are, where they live, what they do.

Paradoxically, that may well be how they like it, unconsciously how they planned it. Robin has

Above: Young cheeses are racked and turned at regular intervals to assist blueing and ripening. Opposite top: Gary and Elise Jungheim outside Country Cheeses Tavistock and below. Like Roquefort, Beenleigh and the other blues are wrapped in foil before they are sold.

reached the stage where he could sell more cheese: it's sold worldwide even if it isn't a household name in Totnes High Street. He doesn't want to. Nor is he thinking of retiring to Tuscany or the Dordogne.

Nick referred to him as 'an old curmudgeon', but with a warmth that radiates from Ticklemore Farm. It has the subcutaneous feel of a working commune. Within its boundaries, it runs on a cantankerous kind of idealism. When one of the helpers forgot to inoculate the milk with the blueing bacteria, it would have been a sacking offence in a conventional factory. Here, it was a minor accident that could be shrugged off. Robin has buried enough of his own spoiled cheeses in the past. In any event there were probably enough *Penicillium* spores floating around the ripening room for the cheeses to blue naturally once they had been spiked.

Pleasures of the Pannier Market

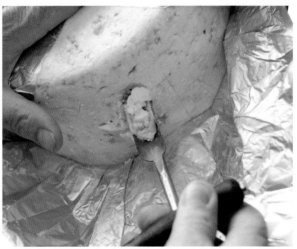

Nose round any Devonshire town. Sooner rather than later you will find the pannier market. It takes its name from the basket that was once used to carry bread. Some of them are scruffy or run down. Some like Barnstaple's are architectural gems. Tavistock's on the fringe of Dartmoor, a grey limestone arsenal of a building gifted to the town by the 7th Duke of Bedford in the 1850s, dominates the centre. In the protective skin of the small shops surrounding it, Gary and Elise Jungheim's Country Cheeses does something that would have been impossible a generation ago. It sells exclusively British cheeses, something that only Neal's Yard Dairy in Covent Garden can claim to do.

Gary and Elise Jungheim, the owners, encourage the good burghers of Tavistock to sample their wares with a passion and enthusiasm verging on the theatrical. They generate such a hum of excitement around them that five minutes at their counter would prove a heady fix for the most jaded retail junky.

Gary's mother, Hazel, started the business, selling six cheeses from a table in the pannier market's main hall. She had heard about Rachel Stephens' Curworthy and was astounded to learn that none was being sold in the town, a gap she was determined to plug. It didn't seem right to her that nearly all the region's produce was sent to London, and that those who should have had first access to it were blissfully ignorant of its existence. When she fell ill, Elise and Gary took over. The numbers of cheeses they stocked crept up to twenty. They moved first to a cubby-hole unit and, early in the 1990s, to the current premises.

147

By focusing on British cheeses and refusing to stock foreign ones, however tempting that might have been from a commercial standpoint, they grew closer to the cheesemakers supplying them. From the outset, Gary felt a special regard for Robin Congdon of Beenleigh and Ticklemore cheese: 'I found him wonderfully interesting. I thought this bloke was a bit of a god, because everything milky he touches turns into golden cheese. I believe that he has curdy fingers just like some gardeners have green ones.'

From their position as inquisitive learners, Elise and Gary have gained in stature to the extent that they act as a cross between ambassadors and impresarios for the cheeses they stock. They are on first-name terms with the makers supplying them. They understand the craftsmanship that has gone into the cheeses they stock, while being only too well aware that the individuals responsible for making them are often isolated, may have little idea what else is available, and have a sketchy sense of what the public enjoys.

They take the view that if someone is passionate about his or her own cheese and knows that it hits the spot, they don't need to suss out the competition. It's their job to sell it. However, newcomers don't become experts overnight. They need feedback. For instance, Elise sampled a promising Old Burford soft cheese with a silky texture, but found the taste too salty. That information will filter back to the maker. A small adjustment would deal with a problem that might prevent it from adding to the growing diaspora of speciality cheeses.

Because what matters most to them is always the flavour, they never let themselves be swayed by appearance. They would far rather serve a ripe Sharpham spilling over the back of the counter to their customers than a firmer one that would display itself better and be easier to cut. According to Gary: 'Any difficulty over its looks is repaid twice over when you eat it. There are too many fine restaurants that worry about presentation and I'd say to them don't worry about getting it onto the plate in a fine little wedge. If you have to spoon it on the plate do so, because that's the business.'

'Soft and runny cheese', he admitted, can make the hairs prickle on the back of his neck. To him, they are 'emotive', so much so that he commissioned Debbie Mumford at Sharpham to make Celeste, a smaller extra-gooey version of Elmhirst and a goats' cheese, Bakesey Meadow, named after a field at the back of his home: 'We've actually got little wooden boxes for it so it can be put in the box, ripened right up till liquid and then with the top split open dipped into. It's like eating nectar.'

Comparing Elise and Gary's approach to handling cheese and that of, say, Waitrose, a supermarket chain that works hard to provide speciality British cheese in its stores, is like measuring a couture dress against an off-the-peg one. The chain, even with the best will, has to standardise its offer. It may ask the cheesemaker to change the firmness or the ripeness or the packaging. Country Cheeses pushes in the other direction. It welcomes the seasonal variations, encourages experiments, takes a chance, on the basis of a gut feeling. Where the multiple would expect its nettle-wrapped Cornish Yarg to be young, bright and green, Gary and Elise want it aged until it's 'Black and rusty and the paper sticks to it and you know that it's good.'

The couple ordered forty Lincolnshire Poacher hard cheeses that had been aged for twenty-eight months (it's normally aged for a year or so) for no good reason other than that they loved the taste. The last of it could be three years old or more before it's eaten, but it will still taste powerful and delicious.

When Country Cheeses pinned the British colours to its mast and refused to buy from overseas, it was dependent on an insignificant little industry with some modest products. Now, as a cheesemonger, it can compete on equal terms with any continental *fromager*. Gary and Elise buy the best, handle it with care and share their pleasure unstintingly with their customers.

Nobody Inn

The Nobody Inn, a whitewashed pub a few miles from Exeter has become an institution in the South West for its wines (about 800 on the list at the last count), whiskies (bought in casks) and cheeses. Nick Borst-Smith was one of the first landlords to buy cheese direct from the makers, discovering Sharpham, Ticklemore and Curworthy. Today, aspiring cheesemakers still bring their wares for him to test.

Because cheese figures strongly on his menus, not least for its ability to mix with wines: 'A light Australian Muscat with Beenleigh Blue is heaven', his chefs are encouraged to cook up new recipes with any that may come along.

Caramelised Onion and Beenleigh Blue Cheese and Rosemary Tart

Serves 8   Wine suggestion: Alsatian Pinot Blanc

115g butter (preferably Denhay)
2 finely sliced large onions
4 sprigs chopped fresh rosemary
1 large pastry shell, baked blind
225g blue cheese (Beenleigh Blue)
6 organic eggs
900ml single cream

Pre-heat the oven to 170°C/350°F/Gas Mark 4. Fry the onions in the butter until nicely browned. Add the rosemary. Spread the mixture over the base of the pastry shell and scatter crumbled cheese over the top. Beat the eggs and cream together and pour into the shell. Place in the oven and bake for 45 minutes.

Beetroot Tarte Tatin with Balsamic Vinegar and Vulscombe Goats' Cheese

Serves 4   Wine suggestion: New World Pinot Noir

115g butter
2 finely sliced large onions
6 thinly sliced cooked baby beetroots
220g puff pasty
60g Vulscombe goats' cheese (or Rosary)
1tsp Balsamic vinegar

Pre-heat the oven to 200°C/400°F/Gas Mark 6. Fry the onions in half the butter until soft. Melt the rest of the butter and coat the slices of beetroot with it. Layer them in a frying pan without a handle and cover with the onions. Roll out the puff pastry to the size of the pan and trim to fit. Place over the top; transfer the pan to the oven and cook for 15–20 minutes. Turn out onto a plate, beetroot side up. Cover the top with finely sliced Vulscombe cheese (you need to cut with a wire) and drizzle with Balsamic vinegar.

The Sharpham Syndrome

Up hill, down dale, the South Hams rises and falls, green like some idealised Middle Earth landscape. An invisible magnet, it attracts society's intentional and accidental escapees. It's a natural home of the Liberty Cap and the Hopi Candle, Cheirology, Vortex Healing and Reiki, or, at another level, the Dartington College of Arts, Rudolph Steiner School and a centre for Buddhist Studies.

If any English region can be described as self-sufficient, this is it, not because it grows all its corn, but because it has a community of taste. There are probably few statistics to back the assertion, but probably more locally produced organic foods are grown or reared here per head of the population than anywhere else in the country. 'Shares in bio-dynamic beef? You got it'; subscription to the largest vegetable box scheme in Britain? Riverford Farm runs it. Even the non-organic South Devon Chilli Farm makes a point of removing greenfly from its peppers by hand. What it does next with them might concern local Buddhists, but few gardeners.

The Sharpham estate doesn't even think it worthwhile to mention the fact that its eponymous cheese is organic. It doesn't have to. One of the earliest mould-ripened cheeses to be made in Britain, its colour, taste and texture do the necessary talking.

Opposite: The River Dart winds its way past the Sharpham estate.
Right: The Sharpham estate was set up by the philanthropic planner Maurice Ash.

The farm, rolling down to a tight loop in the River Dart, two miles out of Totnes by the footpath, perhaps four by road, is a swathe of idyllic pasture and knots of ancient broadleaf trees.

When the economist Maurice Ash bought the estate in 1961, moving from Essex with a herd of Jersey cows, he was taking on a rundown farm that offered little prospect of making him a richer man. Judging by the grey Palladian mansion that went with the sale, designed by Sir Robert Taylor who also designed the façade of the Bank of England – massive rather than elegant – this may not have been his priority. Though wealthy, he didn't fit the typical landowning stereotype. An early environmentalist, he felt that the landed gentry who swallowed up the great estates after the Dissolution of the Monasteries by Henry VIII had failed in their duty of stewardship towards the countryside. He leaned towards the medieval model where land owned by the church had been the focus of a rural life that both supported and was sustained by spiritual communities. It was a holistic view that stressed the fusion between material and inner experience.

Idealism apart, it was probably something more banal, the slump in milk prices in the 1970s, that pushed him towards setting up a cheesemaking dairy. It did, though, fit with his convictions. Modern commodity-led agriculture had systematically stripped away the need for rural workers. By making cheese on the estate he would win back a skilled job to the farm. At exactly the same time, he planted the first vines of a vineyard that has been nurtured to provide grapes for some of the most exciting wines in Britain.

The lord of the manor set about his new initiatives like a true 'Southhamsian'. Vines were being planted all over southern England, but the grape varieties chosen were almost exclusively German, because accepted wisdom had it that the climate was too cold to plant French ones. Ash decided to follow his own francophile instincts and put in Pinot Noir, the classic Burgundian *cepage* and Madeleine Angevine, a grape related to the Muscat that ripens early in the summer and is eaten in France but never pressed for wine.

His plans for his Jersey milk were equally eccentric. He didn't want to make a hard cheese, but he did like Brie, so that was what he decided to go ahead with. Nobody in Britain was doing it, nor had he taken the advice of the experts from the Ministry of Agriculture. They insisted, with all the scientific facts at their fingertips, that the

Above: Mark Sharman (centre) with his wine-making team.
Opposite: Sharpham's wines are regularly voted among the finest in the country.

'If I do not drink wine, may I drink water with cheese?' Never. Not even with mild cheeses. Water and cheese together can cause stomach-ache. Better take no cheese at all if you do not take a drink that is slightly alcoholic. Another possibility is to take the cheese and drink nothing.

From *Guide du Fromage* by Pierre Androuët

globules of fat in Channel Island milk were too large to produce a soft cheese. His response was to send a Polish girl, Isa Caroll, his dairymaid-in-waiting, to a farmhouse Brie maker in central France to learn how it was done there. Had he realised it, Normandy cows produce milk that's

not unlike Jerseys and it hasn't ever prevented the making of Camembert.

Isa returned to open a dairy in a converted stable. Her early attempts could, according to those who sampled them, be 'sublime'. On the other hand, they had a habit of ripening so fast that the slippery cheese might come running out from its *Penicillium candidum* overcoat the moment it was cut, making it impossible for cheesemongers to portion. Despite the rejects, almost everyone lucky enough to try it knew that it had a special quality.

Meanwhile, Mark Sharman, a young engineer who had been mining for gold in Canada and had returned to England to manage a cousin's orchard along the Dart Valley near Dittisham, was engaged to take on the budding vineyard.

Now managing the estate and a partner of the trust that Maurice Ash set up before he died, Mark recalled that he taught himself the rudiments as he went along: 'I learned on the hoof, but having been a fruit grower I could transfer the knowledge of pruning and weed control but not to the wine making.'

He filled this gap by attending the first winemaking course held in England at Plumpton in Sussex, travelling to the college for three weeks then returning to tend to his vines.

While he was still settling in, his first vintage not yet under his belt, Isa informed Maurice Ash that she was going to stop making Sharpham in order to marry. At this juncture one of those serendipitous chains of events that happen in the South Hams took place. There were probably less than a hundred artisan cheesemakers in Britain at that time. One of them, Robin Congdon, was making Beenleigh in the neighbouring hamlet down river. His assistant, Debbie Mumford, happened to be Mark's partner.

It was agreed that she would move to Sharpham to be trained for two months by Isa before she left, and that afterwards Robin would keep a watching brief over the dairy until Debbie was confident enough to take over.

Also in true South Hams fashion, things didn't work out quite as planned. After spending a day under Isa's supervision, Debbie was told by her that she knew how to make cheese, wouldn't have any more problems and wouldn't require any more help. Isa's departure changed the whole outlook at the Sharpham estate. Imbued with the Totnes spirit, Isa had liked to take an annual three-month break from her duties. Routine never suited her. According to Mark, she still lives in Totnes, intermittently selling amber imported from her native Poland in the town's pannier market.

Perhaps Sharpham cheese, lacking her artistic touch, changed as a result of her departure. It was less temperamental, but that was probably down to Robin's suggestion that the milk should be thermised. This halfway house of heat-treating, in between

leaving the milk raw and pasteurising it, gives a measure of security and consistency. How much it may alter the character is debatable, but it won't prevent a skilled craftsman working with the right raw material from turning out an excellent cheese.

And nobody has ever questioned whether Sharpham is that. Richer than a French Brie de Meaux or its cousin the Brie de Melun, maybe sweeter too, less powerful than either, it stands out from the rank and file factory 'Brie-toos', that are often well made though lacking personality.

Having absorbed and digested Robin's tyrological wisdom, Debbie was making more

Sharpham's than had ever been done previously. She also introduced a new cheese to the dairy. Elmhirst, the maiden name of Ash's wife, has an almost mythical standing in and around Totnes. Her father, Leonard, secretary of the Indian poet and thinker, Rabindranath Tragore had married Dorothy, heiress to the Whitney fortune, one of the richest women in the world. Together they had set up the Dartington Hall Trust in the 1920s, rescuing a medieval hall, putting up buildings, developing the 1,000-acre estate with landscape gardening, forestry and farming, creating studios and workshops for arts and crafts, and starting a world-famous school which was considered,

Opposite: Jersey cows are the key to the richness of Sharpham's cheeses.

according to taste, progressive and enlightened or shocking and depraved.

The mould-ripened cheese has a certain opulence about it, too, down to the extra cream that is added. It's difficult to handle. The fresh junket isn't cut up in the vat like most cheeses and it's ladled by hand into the moulds without being drained. Eaten young, after two or three weeks, it has an open texture, neither chalky like some under-ripe soft cheeses, nor crumbly, nor smooth and melting like the Brillat-Savarin that was created by the Parisian Master Cheesemonger, Henri Androuët. It's fresh and clean-tasting, but develops more body and a more cultured-buttery flavour given an extra fortnight's aging.

Rustic, Debbie's next initiative, has the outer appearance of a large flattened snowball. The experts may dispute whether it's semi-hard or semi-soft, but the difficulty of defining it comes from it being an original, not comparable to other cheeses. It has a refreshing, light tang to it that balances the milk's fatness. It's almost touching that it should marry well with the pale-lemon tints, dried-lower taste and refreshing finish of Mark's Madeleine Angevine. Being whimsical, it's satisfying – and perhaps implausible – to imagine the two of them picnicking on bread, wine and cheese by the riverside on a warm summer's day.

They do almost work side by side. At the outset, the dairy was at the estate's entrance, separated from the winery by a road that meandered through the property. Because the cheese side outgrew the stables it was moved to a new site beside the hangar where Mark makes wine. It's tempting to compare the skills both require. Both start with a liquid and rely on the process of fermentation. The big contrast between them is that Debbie starts afresh every day, whereas Mark has one vintage a year to make it all happen. That is not strictly true,

because he will produce several wines over a period lasting a month, but it does underline how two ingredients, both more than ninety per cent water to begin with, can end up completely different from each other.

Maurice Ash died in 2003, but his ghost would probably approve of the way in which the Sharmans have in a matter-of-fact way lived up to his ideals. The herd that he had brought with him always supplied more milk than was needed by the dairy. It wasn't strictly organic either. The old Sharpham leys were picturesque but poor grazing. Now the pasturage has been improved with the sowing of new grasses, borage and plantain. The cattle are reared completely organically, although Mark has shied from approaching the Soil Association. Most significant is maintaining the balance between the milk they furnish and the amount Debbie needs. It establishes a virtuous cycle that is a key to sustainable agriculture.

Although orders for Sharpham keep rolling in, it's not something that Mark or Debbie would undermine. Nor would they have the opportunity of doing so, should they want to. In 1984 Maurice Ash had formed a trust that would oversee the separate operations carried out on his property, but allow each one to run itself. The house became the College for Buddhist Studies & Contemporary Enquiry. Cheese - and winemaking were later fused into the Sharpham Partnership. Its three tenanted farms had to be compatible with the aims that underpinned his ambition: 'To maintain, conserve and enhance the land, buildings, resources and bio-diversity of its estate for public benefit.'

It's a benevolent, almost altruistic dictatorship, it could be argued, like that imposed by the great feudal abbeys, which Ash so much admired. And, as Mark testifies, it does not seek to crush personal initiative: 'Debbie and I are both independent, stubborn, single-minded. That's how you make good wine or cheese.'

Sharpham Wines and Cheeses

The Sharpham estate owes its existence to idealism rather than any slow but continuous evolution in a rural landscape. It can't be likened to any particular corner of France, Italy or Spain where both produce and products have developed over generations in tandem, shaped by the climate, the soil and the people. Channel Island cows supplying milk for hybrid cheeses can coexist with wine made from French grapes grown on the same Devonshire property. They don't always make ideal partners. Sometimes the two may clash. A mouthful of rich, fatty Sharpham cheese will flatten the fresh, floral finish of a Madeleine Angevine wine made from vines that were planted in the original vineyard.

Luckily, the choice of both wines and cheeses has developed. Mark took over five acres of vines, planted on one of the steepest slopes overlooking the Dart. Learning by experience, he expanded the vineyard to sixteen acres, before cutting back to ten, in the process removing much of the earliest planting that were not only hard to manage, but provided disappointing fruit.

At the outset, the winery concentrated on white wines. Now it consistently wins Best English Red Wine with either its Sharpham Pinot Noir or Beenleigh Red, made at the winery with Cabernet Sauvignon and Merlot grapes from a tiny, one-acre sister vineyard of Mark's.

Should cheese be matched to wine or vice versa? It's a 'chicken and egg' situation that doesn't have a ready answer. It all depends on the context. Good as they are, there's no call to genuflect before opening a bottle of Sharpham's white, sparkling or rosé wines, but they will be spoiled by eating a cheese that doesn't suit them. The reds, for most of us, will be tied to what is being eaten as a main course. In this instance it's more a question of choosing the cheese that will complement the final glass.

Rustic or Rustic with chives. These mild young, semi-hards aren't just the best Sharpham cheeses to enjoy with the white wines made on the estate, they are the only ones that work.

Choose: Sharpham Estate Selection Dry (100 per cent Madeleine Angevine), Dart Valley Reserve (light, dry, floral, reminiscent of dry Muscat), Sharpham Barrel Fermented Dry.

Ticklemore. Sharpham cheesemaker Debbie Mumford makes these open-textured, semi-hard goats' cheeses for Sarie Cooper and Robin Congdon. It's his recipe, but he stopped making it because his own blue cheeses interfered with the ripening.

Choose: Sharpham Rosé (it's made from the German Dornfelder grape that gives a fruity and aromatic wine), Sharpham Red (also made from Dornfelder).

Sharpham. Cheeses of the Brie family hold their own with elegant or racy red wines. Because Sharpham is so rich, it would help to eat some good crusty bread with it. For a summer barbecue the Sharpham Red would be pleasant, while the Beenleigh Red is more of a dinner party match.

Choose: Sharpham Red, Beenleigh Red (Cabernet Sauvignon, Merlot).

Elmhirst. This is a very rich, mould-ripened cheese that has a moussy, open texture when it starts to mature and becomes progressively more gooey from the rind towards the centre.

Choose: Sharpham Pinot Noir (on the nose its style is closer to French Burgundies than the New World Pinot Noirs, but it has a silky mouth feel and intense flavours of ripe fruit and spice).

Celeste. Debbie Mumford makes this Camembert-sized cheese exclusively for Country

Creamy Sharpham cheese on sale at Bath Fine Cheese Co.

Cheeses, Tavistock. The recipe is similar to Elmhirst, but the cheese is ripened like a Camembert to give the same silky texture.

Choose: Sharpham Red, Sharpham Pinot Noir, Beenleigh Red.

Sharpham makes modern wine that is ready for drinking within two years. The quality doesn't vary much between vintages because of the vineyard's location close to the Dart, which protects it against extremes of hot and cold weather. Other wines include New Release, a dry, white, new season wine and Sharpham Sparkling, made from Pinot Noir and Kernling grapes.

157

1 and 2: Debbie Mumford ladles the curds into the mould by hand when making a delicate triple cream Elmhirst.

3 Up to her elbows in cream!

4 Ticklemore cheese made by sharpham for Robin Congdon.

5 Harp knives have parallel blades to cut the curd.

6 The curd is brind before ripening.

7 Young cheese will soon be swathed in a penicillium candidum coating.

8 Portioning cheese before setting it to ripen.

Nettle Cheese

Transport Lynher Dairy by some sci-fi teleporting system from Pengreep Farm near Truro to a piece of Californian woodland and it would stand out as a stylish New Age boutique cheesemaking facility. Its slimline timber cladding disguises the industrial frame. Environmentally friendly, it recycles energy from its chilling system to heat water, which is then filtered after use through a reed-bed system that cleanses it and feeds it into a flourishing wildlife pond. In the two years after being built, the dairy scooped three separate architectural prizes including a Civic Trust Award (2003) for the best UK agricultural building.

This is the current home of Yarg, a mythical-sounding Cornish cheese that is little more than twenty years old. It owes its popularity to a stinging-nettle wrapping that does as much for the imagination of those eating it as for any particular flavour it derives from the leaves.

Allegedly it traces its pedigree back to an early-seventeenth-century best seller, *The English Housewife* by Gervase Markham, when freshly made cheeses were called either 'white meats' or 'green cheese' and were sometimes laid out on nettles while they aged. A possible explanation for why nettles were used is that dairymaids believed it would hasten the cheeses' maturation. Laying plums between layers of nettles to ripen them was a common rural wheeze. If this seems curious, what should we think about Italians who wrapped cheeses they exported to Germany in tree bark at about the same period?

Speculation aside, the unvarnished story doesn't make the hairs on the back of the neck stand on end. Allan Gray, a local ecologist, who was experimenting with a kind of Caerphilly, found the reference and started slapping nettles around young cheese. Looking for premises to make the cheese he approached Michael Horrell a tenant farmer on the Duchy of Cornwall estate who was able to convert an unused building on his farm into a dairy, and the two men formed a partnership. When Gray's enthusiasm lagged, he sold his recipe and a client list that included the improbably named Rustic Egg and Cheese Company, Brixton, to his partner.

Using milk from his herd, Michael turned a folksy product into a viable one, creating one of the few artisan cheeses that have outgrown their hand-crafted beginnings. When Michael realised that he couldn't meet the demand from his own farm, he went into partnership with another farming couple, Ben and Catherine Mead. At the outset, and probably against all the tenets of business practice, Yarg was being made in their two dairies. Now it's only made in the new Lynher Dairy *factory*.

If this word conjures up stainless steel, high-performance machinery and systems management, it's appropriate. So, too, is the earlier meaning of the word that is linked to the Italian *fattoria,* a farm where produce is transformed. Although the way Yarg is made is substantially the same as how Allan Gray did it, it's been tweaked and tinkered with, for instance, to take account of changes in the milk between summer and winter.

After the starter and vegetarian rennet have been added to the milk, the curd is cut into

Opposite: Catherine Mead, Yarg's new nettle queen.
Right: Many tons of nettles are hand-picked each year to wrap around the cheese.

pea-sized gobbets and stirred for forty-five minutes until they firm up. Cut up three more times and the whey drained off, the curd is shredded through a mill and pressed overnight before brining. Left to dry off, it's ready for its nettle overcoat. Decked out, the cheese goes into the store where (turned every day) it ripens, developing a lightly mottled bloom of moulds during the two months it remains there before being shipped out.

When it's first ready for eating, sliced like a cake, it's still a bit crumbly, but it firms up with a little extra ageing. Then the combination of mould and leaves give it a mild but pleasant fungal flavour that balances the cheese's natural sour-dough acidity. There's a hint of bitterness, too, but that may be down to the vegetarian rennet used to curdle the milk. More than a few 'experts' have picked out a spinachy taste. There may be, but it could also be the eye and the mind playing tricks with the taste buds. 'Vegetal', another common description, covers a wide range of possibilities. 'Smoky' and 'artichoke' – how a Californian farmstead cheesemaker with its own take on a nettle cheese

Like Caerphilly to which it's related, Yarg is soaked in brine before being coated in nettles.

refers to the aromas – may be pushing it. Probably the fairest analysis would be that Yarg tastes green because the brain says that it ought to.

Each year there's a window of about six weeks beginning in May when the nettles, only the common kind, not the purple or white-flowered dead nettles, nor the related Yellow Archangel, are picked. The season comes, conveniently for the gangs of mainly Central European pickers, at the end of the daffodil harvest and before they lift the bulbs. In this window of opportunity, they will collect over three tonnes of the leaves that have to be gathered in pristine condition and of a certain minimum size.

Lynher Dairy has experimented with rarer red hemp nettles that in large doses can be mildly toxic to livestock and has commissioned studies into growing nettles as a cash crop, but the wild 'stingers' are still its basic raw material.

Brought to the dairy they are washed, packed in stacks with their veins up and deep-frozen. Each cheese is veneered with leaves by hand. Defrosting renders them pliable and sting-free. They stick easily to the fresh curd. A ring of symmetrical dragon's teeth goes around the side. Then its top is covered, before being turned upside down and the process reversed. When wrapped, Yarg looks like a deep green sawn-off seven-pound log.

Despite the work that has gone into regularising it, it's still a labour-intensive artisan product that may change seasonally in colour and body. The nettles, too, will alter the maturing depending on whether they've been collected early or late in the season. Yarg can also be customised for privileged customers. Neal's Yard Dairy takes a larger cheese made with an animal rennet, that Lynher's chief maker, Dane Hopkins, says he prefers. He has experimented with assorted vegetation as a covering, rejecting most because they don't work.

An exception has been the Wild Garlic Yarg.

Allium ursinum grows abundantly in Cornwall's woodlands, emerging early in the year with the snowdrops. Its broad, lance-shaped leaves have long been popular as a wild food, tasting milder than the cultivated bulbs. The cheese, made to the same recipe as its nettle sister, is ready to eat when it's younger, after five weeks, but the characteristic taste is pleasant and persistent, less aggressive than the garlic cream cheeses.

Dane had worked previously for the now defunct Peverstone Cheese Company at Cullompton, which had been the home of one of the earliest speciality cheeses, Devon Garland, a semi-hard with a distinctive band of herbs, running through the middle. He has adapted this to invent a flecked Cornish Garland (echoing its own early days Lynher now owns the rights to Devon Garland) and another Peverstone-inspired recipe, Tiskey, that has an Italianate thread of sun-dried tomatoes, oregano and basil through its middle.

Instead of moving a few wheels a week to the Rustic Egg and Cheese Company, and hoping to find a wholesaler or grocer's to take a few more, Lynher Dairy measures its weekly output in tonnes. Its customers are the supermarket leviathans with

increasing appetites. After tagging on to theirs, a swelling order book from the USA and Canada, the Yarg phenomenon doesn't seem to be a cottage industry curiosity so much as a small national brand.

In the process it has created the kind of integrated farming business that creates work in a rural area where jobs outside of seasonal tourism are hard to come by without compromising the integrity of what it has to offer.

It's a small and almost forgotten detail of dairy industry history that in 1938, the year before the outbreak of the Second World War, farmers received two separate payments for milk under a scheme as bizarre as any dreamt up by Brussels bureaucrats. They were paid 14 old pence per gallon for liquid milk and only sixpence for manufacturing milk. The regulator, the Milk Board, made the annual assessment as to how much was needed for each of the two uses. So, if it deemed that 70 per cent was needed for drinking and 30 per cent for, say, butter and cheese, then a farmer was paid the corresponding amounts, regardless of his milk's quality. If Britain imported more cheese and butter from the USA or the Commonwealth and made less of its own, the farmers would be better off. It's little wonder then that cheesemaking was so unpopular with producers that it nearly died out on farms after the war. What the independent modern cheesemaker, like Lynher has done, is reconnect the links between the cow, its raw material and the use to which this is put. It gives a higher value to the milk from its herds, than those farmers who look no further than the tanker disappearing up the lane with their daily untraceable, subsidised quota swilling around in its belly. It hasn't lost contact with the core difference that distinguishes a true artisan cheese. Individual care counts for more than speed or any putative efficiency.

Getting off One's Tuffet

Little Miss Muffet sat on a tuffet,
Eating her curds and whey.
There came a big spider and sat down beside her
And frightened Miss Muffet away.

Who was the young lady? Where was she sitting? What was she eating? The last question is the easiest to answer. When rennet is added to milk, it forms a gel – a junket – the precursor of cheese that was once a popular snack sweetened and dusted with nutmeg. The impressionable girl may (and this is a speculation of those who try to unravel the secret meanings of nursery rhymes) have been the daughter of the entomologist Thomas Moufet, author of *Insectorum Theatrum* (1634), the first published attempt at cataloguing the insect world. The 'tuffet' is the most mysterious element of the three. It could be an early form of 'tuft' or it could be a low stool. Nobody, least of all the dictionary, is quite sure.

This roundabout introduction to cheesemaker, Sue Proudfoot, can be justified on the grounds that she named a cheese after the rhyme's heroine. It's doubly so, because she has the kind of gritty attitude that always confronts trouble rather than runs from it. Cheese mites in her storeroom might possibly cause her concern, but she'd deal with them. Scared of spiders? No way.

Opposite: Whalesborough Farm overlooks the spectacular North Cornwall coastline.
Above: Sue Proudfoot shows off her Trelawny, Miss Muffet and Keltic Gold cheeses.

Whalesborough Farm, chunky, imposing, built to last, stands a mile from the rocky North Cornwall coast midway between Bude and Boscastle. Its long granite barn and outbuildings do justice to the 500 acres of woods and pasture making up the property. And like many other Cornish farms the impression of agricultural permanence is a virtual reality. There's no herd of dairy cattle grazing the fields, secure inside picturesque dry-stone walls. Instead, there are cottage conversions (with a heated swimming-pool) to attract incomers in

search of rugged scenery and outdoor pursuits, provided that there's comfort, too. A forty-foot climbing tower fills a converted grain silo and the barn houses a bouldering centre for rock climbers.

When Sue first started, her husband Fraser still ran a dairy herd. The couple had met at Cirencester Agriculture College, in the days when lecturers didn't teach farming students that their future lay in barn conversions or that gastrotourism was going to play a key role in the future of the countryside. It was a period when, if they listened to *The Archers,* 'an everyday story of country folk', wives might toy with the idea of making yoghurt or, if they happened to be in Cornwall, clotted cream.

This is what she did initially, in a dairy that was little more than a shed. It was just one of a series of

UK, which was coming bottom of the European league in terms of payments.

With £3,000 savings behind her, she set about scrubbing down the old dairy that had once produced clotted cream and converting it for cheesemaking. Her problem was that she didn't know how to proceed: 'My mother met someone in Somerfield who knew someone who was something to do with cheese.' That backdoor introduction led to her meeting a microbiologist and cheesemaker who had experience developing cheese recipes for 10,000-litre creamery vats. He spent two days at Whalesborough in 1999 teaching her a recipe. Instead of a press, they made do with tractor wheels.

From there to selling at Lostwithiel Farmers' Market involved all the exasperation and soul-searching that seems to haunt every newcomer to cheesemaking: 'The worst thing is selling something when you aren't sure whether it's good or not. It's much harder to undo a bad reputation than establish a good one.'

She feared, too, that the Environmental Health Officer who inspected her dairy would close her down, or tell her to change the way she worked. Instead she found him sympathetic, someone who could distinguish between her real concern for avoiding food safety hazards and the cosmetic appearance of her shack-like facility.

From the outset she pasteurised the milk, partly because tuberculosis is a serious problem in Cornwall, but principally because, as an apprentice, she didn't want to add a level of risk. It hasn't been a constraint. Although cheesemonger Stephen Gunn, of the Truro Cheese Shop, encouraged her to switch because of his conviction that unpasteurised always adds complexity to the taste as well as being more easily assimilated by the digestive system, it's not certain that a change of

money-making ventures she tackled. Another was hawking free-range eggs around Bude in a child's pushchair. For a while she bred and reared a flock of pedigree Bleu du Maine sheep, a fashionable breed introduced from northern France. In other incarnations, she worked as a classroom assistant for children with special needs, a co-ordinator for the Federation of Young Farmers and a talented painter of milk churns.

Cheese, though, isn't a stopgap means of supplementing income. It rarely is with those who are hooked. It may have begun using milk from her husband's herd, but it has survived its demise, a victim of the waves of badger-born tuberculosis, BSE and foot-and-mouth disease that have rolled over north Cornish farmers like the Atlantic breakers. Nor did it help that the Duchy's farmers received less for their milk than elsewhere in the recipe would improve cheeses that already have character. Nor has his personal preference prevented him from shepherding her through the development of the small cylinders of Keltic Gold, cured in cider that he sold at his shop as the Cheese with No Name.

The first crisis came when Fraser gave up his herd. Sue solved it by approaching a neighbouring organic dairy farm. Helsett Farm lies in the lee of a hill above the tiny harbour of Boscastle. Here, Sarah Ponsonby-Talbot with her daughter Eila make a clotted cream ice-cream that has the richness and concentrated flavour that comes from working on a tiny scale with

no compromises to commercial practice. The basis for this is the organic herd of pedigree Ayrshire cattle. They not only produce richer milk, but it's lower in cholesterol than other breeds.

Helsett had a surplus of milk. By delivering directly to Sue, Helsett created a kind of ideal collaboration between two specialised businesses, both operating on a shoestring, both aspiring to work to the highest quality. Whether it was strictly legal in the red-tape burdened environment of modern agriculture is questionable, but in France or Italy small producers in a similar position would just go

A Cornish Cheesecake

This is based on a Jewish recipe from the food writer Clarissa Hyman whose deli-owning grandparents from Manchester survived the *Titanic*. It's Cornish in that it relies on a fresh cream cheese from Toppenrose Dairy called Trenance Softee that is both suave and rich.

For the base:
150g self-raising flour
pinch of salt
75g caster sugar
75g cubed unsalted butter
½tsp vanilla extract
1 medium–large egg, beaten

For the filling:
750g Trenance Softee
150g caster sugar
50g cornflour
150ml soured cream
3 eggs, separated
4tbs seeded raisins
10ml lemon juice

Line either a 22cm cake tin with a moveable base or a spring-form tin with baking parchment.

For the pastry dough, sift the flour and salt. Add the sugar. Rub in the butter until the mixture looks like breadcrumb. Combine with the vanilla and egg and work into a smooth ball. Rest 30 minutes. Roll out the pastry to about 30cm diameter between clingfilm. Cut out a circle to fit the base of the tin and lay over the parchment.

Preheat the oven to 180°C/350°F/ gas mark 4.

For the filling, beat the cheese, sugar, cornflour, soured cream and egg yolks together until smooth. Fold in the raisins. Whisk the egg whites and lemon juice until well risen and they hold their shape on the whisk. Fold the whites into the cheese mixture with a spatula or metal spoon. Pour into over the pastry base. Bake for seventy-five minutes. Leave to cool in the oven with the door ajar. Don't try to turn out the cheesecake until it is cold.

ahead, secure that no officious bureaucrat would bother them.

It was a tenuous situation though, one that could leave Sue without her raw material were the source to vanish. Milk Link, the industry giant that buys Cornish farm milk, stipulates that its customers must not supply third parties. Sue would be able to buy from them, except that she needs a few hundred litres, not the 20,000 that their lorries deliver. It's an irony, because the business was set up as a farmers' co-operative, whose aim was to serve the interests of the farming community.

The Ayrshire milk was bringing an extra dimension to Sue's cheeses. Unfortunately, Milk Link dug in and prevented Helsett from supplying her. As a compromise, though it replaced the source that had dried up with milk from its own nominated farms. The change caused her more problems initially but she has learnt to live with them. Her original, truckle-sized Trelawny, isn't too distant from a medium cheddar, or wasn't when it was

conceived. It has changed, becoming more buttery in the mouth, round, with a pleasant lemony tang. Its texture is also moister because it's pressed more lightly like some American hard cheeses related to cheddar, but still has plenty of body.

The Miss Muffet has a springiness and cleanness on the palate, like the best Dutch Edams and Goudas but without the synthetic feel that some of the factory varieties have. It's made to a 'washed-curd' recipe. After the whey has been drained from the vat, the curd is rinsed with water before being pressed. This produces what some cheesemakers refer to as a 'sweet body', an expression used to describe a supple flex that doesn't break readily when a plug is taken with a cheese iron and bent end to end.

According to Sue, the hardest thing for the small isolated producer to find out is who is buying what she is making. Of course, she has plum customers such as Fortnum & Mason and Paxton & Whitfield, but mostly she sells through wholesalers that move her cheese into the network of delis, pubs and

Opposite: The barn where her husband used to keep the farm's cattle lies empty.
Right: Hard cheeses threatened by the unsympathetic attitude of Milk Link.

restaurants. Early on, she was visited by Randolph Hodgson of Neal's Yard Dairy and he took the Trelawny and Miss Muffet for a while, although she soon realised that he was in an uniquely privileged position, able to pick and choose from the very best cheese being made at any given moment.

Rather than fight for shelf space in this intensely competitive environment, she decided that she would concentrate on being a regional cheesemaker, focusing on the increasing sophistication of the Duchy. Not so long ago, Cornwall, she argued, was about Wall's ice-cream and cheddar. In the space of a decade it has changed into the county that was voted 'the best place to be if you are a foodie' by *Observer* readers. If that means that the Cornish have turned gastrotourism into a genuine part of what they offer alongside the Eden Project, Tintagel and Land's End, so be it.

Apart from the giant Davidstow creamery owned by Dairy Crest that makes Cathedral City, the leading cheddar brand, the numbers of cheesemakers has risen well into double figures, producing everything from soft goats' cheese balls in herb-scented oil (St Marwenne), Wild Garlic Yarg (Lynher) and Softee (Toppenrose) to Cheetham's Chough and Beast of Bodmin (Toppenrose).

One of the incidental effects of the way the numbers continue to grow like Topsy, is that yesterday's dairymaid can become today's latest fashionable cheesemaker. For two years, Terri Rasmussen worked at Whalesborough. Now, having converted a corrugated-iron barn beside her house overlooking the Tamar Valley, she's making her own Tamaracott ewes' milk cheeses: Baalumi, Baa Humbug and Hobson's Choice. If some of these seem like sheepish takes on recipes she may have gleaned from working with Sue, that's to be

expected. And like Sue, who was and still is glad of any advice she can get, Terri is picking the brains of Stephen Gunn, who can help her with the science as well as advising her as to whether people are going to want to buy it.

To put things in perspective, the Dairy Crest factory probably makes more cheese in a week than all the craft cheesemakers of Cornwall combined can handcraft in a year. It isn't though a question of comparing like with like. Behind Cathedral City is a century of dairy technology directed towards providing ton after ton of a completely consistent product that hundreds of thousands of consumers will buy again and again and again. Sue Proudfoot can only offer cheeses that are an extension of her personality, her best shot on any day, given the combination of unpredictable details that can affect their taste and character.

Blissful Buffalo

'Blissful' is hardly the word Mike Hargreaves or his father Horace would choose to describe their early experiences with buffaloes. 'Frightened me to death', comes nearer to it. Docile they may be once they have settled, but first encounters, especially with beasts that have just arrived on a Devon farm after travelling halfway across Europe from Romania or southern Italy are frankly scary. 'It takes a brave man to milk them', recalled Horace.

Fortunately, or maybe unfortunately, bedding down animals that haven't been seen in the English countryside since the Crusades, assuming they were here then as sources suggest, was relatively simple. Knowing what to do with the milk, that was the real challenge back in the mid-1990s.

Mike's initial thought was to turn it into ice-cream. He had no problem finding a partner to take on the job. The problem, though, was what to call it. Buffalo milk is rich, but it needs extra cream mixed with it to achieve the right level of creaminess. Would it be legal, Mike wondered, to advertise a chocolate chip buffalo milk ice-cream if it relied on cows' cream for its texture? There may have been a semantic solution, but the idea fizzled out.

His next thought was cheese. He sent some of the milk across the border to Cornwall where Caryl Minson, making cheese at Menallack, turned it into

'The distribution of water in Mozzarella cheese differs from most other cheeses due to microstructural differences that result from the stretching process. Microscopic studies have shown that the stretching step during Mozzarella cheese making creates a network of parallel-oriented protein fibers.'

From a scientific paper 'Nuclear Magnetic Resonance Study of Water Mobility in Pasta Filata and Non-Pasta Filata Mozzarella' by Kuo, Johnson and Chen

White Lady, named after Mike's dog (it's called Blissful Buffalo Soft nowadays). Exmoor Blue, another maker, took some for blue cheese. Mike tried his hand and failed at producing a hard cheese of his own. In between, he sold liquid milk and yoghurt.

If this were the whole story, it would paint a picture of an enterprising farmer betting on an outsider and, through his persistence, managing, just, to make the gamble pay off. In effect, his first five years of buffalo farming was a prologue to the moment when he decided to travel, not to Italy but to Holland to learn how mozzarella is made.

It was something of a last resort. Mike had already invited English cheesemaking technologists

Opposite: Buffaloes are 'much more intelligent than cows'.
Below: Mike Hargreaves checks out his stock.

Above: Buffaloes are docile and easy to manage.

and 'experts' who could make hard cheeses blindfold to visit the farm, but they hadn't managed to overcome the difficulty of making a proper, stretchy, elastic curd. 'We didn't know and they didn't know', is how Mike sums up their help.

'We used to heat milk up, put in the starter, try to do this, try to do that and a big lumpy old stuff would come out of the bottom of the vat.'

Mike avoids talking about his experiences in the Netherlands. Whereabouts did he go? He's not saying. Who was his teacher? He can't recall. How did he find him or her? A Dutch lady making cheese in Devon for a goat farmer gave him the contact and, he adds, he did learn from an Italian there.

Even after his return, when he had been shown some of the tricks, he didn't become a master of the art overnight. What he had grasped was the basic technique without which he would never have succeeded: 'You've got to immerse the curd in hot water to be able to stretch it.'

Knowing the how was one thing; learning the practical dexterity that goes with it was something else: 'Even after I'd come home it wasn't very good, not for a long time. It was hard and things like that.'

Mozzarella found its way into the Italian language in 1570 when Bartolomeo Scappi, chef to the Papal court, referred to it in a passage in which he linked it with ricotta, butter and cream. The term *mozza*, standing alone for a cheese is much older. At the Capuan monastery of San Lorenzo, four centuries earlier, monks offered bread and cheese (*mozza o provatura*) to pilgrims. Its meaning, though, refers to a piece that has been pulled or cut off from a whole. It's an apt description of the way in which little lumps of virgin curd are torn from a larger mass.

It's the most famous member of the cheese genus that is now called *pasta filata*. This translates as 'drawn out' pasta or dough. It gives an impression of the elastic strands of curd that behave like well-sucked chewing gum when they are compacted and rolled into a ball. Most culinary

Clockwise, from above left: The curd is cooked before it stretches; it's ready to work when it forms threads; it has to be shaped into a ball; mozzarella is soaked in brine and eaten fresh.

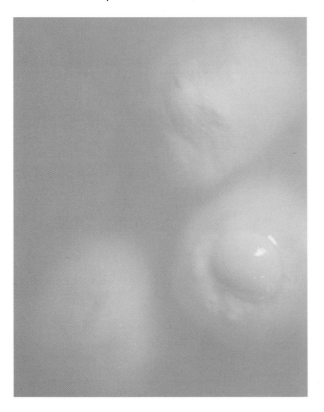

dictionaries represent *filata* as 'spun', which is an alternative, perhaps more common, meaning. That sense is only justifiable when the cheese is heated, for instance on top of a pizza. It's only then that the fine strands are apparent.

Reaching the strung-out stage is one of the trickiest manipulations to test an artisan cheesemaker's skill.

It's a two-man job in which father and son have learned to combine as one, with Horace manhandling the slippery curds and Mike rolling them into plump dumplings. Their dairy is in a converted outbuilding, next door to the butchery where the buffalo meat is cut up and packed. Large enough for a vat in which to coagulate and heat the milk, a paddling-pool in which to drop the freshly formed balls and a stainless steel table wide enough to set two plastic handbasins side by side, it's a far cry from the mozzarella factories

that Mike visited in southern Italy when he went there to study the way farmers rear and feed their livestock.

They keep the door to the yard open. Otherwise the cramped room would be damp and steamy. A side window of panelled glass lets in extra light. The men standing behind their respective bowls face each other.

To follow what happens next, one has to take a step back and trace what has been happening to the milk. As with any other cheese method, it has had a starter and rennet added to it, before the curd is cut into small cubes and the whey drained off. Then it has been left to stew in the vat, heated just above body temperature while more whey seeps out and the curds start to compact. The point of this is to develop the acidity, without which the stringy texture of mozzarella wouldn't be obtained.

Opposite: Mike and Horace show off the team work without which the production of good mozzarella is impossible.
Left: The curd has to be stretched before it is shaped.

In the next hour Mike, wearing powder-blue surgical gloves, has to roll about 300 balls by hand. If he goes any slower, their core will be hard or lumpy, rather than the silky smooth, succulent, squeezy buns that they have to be. Before he can mould them, Horace has to blanch, if that's the right way of describing something that's already DAZ white, in his basin of simmering water. Taking two wooden paddles, he

kneads, lifts and stretches, before sprinkling the curds with a little salt. Only when they're falling off the paddles in matted tresses does the elasticity become apparent.

Mike takes the formed curds, tears off a piece (this is where the 'mozza' part comes in), rolls it deftly and tosses it behind him into the cold-water trough. He would probably feel that his technique is a shortcut or a compromise with the way mozzarella should be made. Before the ball is formed, it may be flattened and folded so that when a cross-section is cut through it, onion-like layers are apparent. For him, the extra step isn't practical.

Serious 'cheesesmiths' class mozzarella as a fresh cheese, which seems vaguely inappropriate in that it has been simmered in water hot enough to poach an egg. Their logic, with which it is hard to quarrel, is that as soon as it's been made it's ready to eat. This is arguably the moment when it's at its best. The scent of fresh buffalo milk is sweet and appetising. The description of the texture, in which it is compared to chicken breast, is apt providing that it's a free-range organic one rather than a factory broiler. The cheese is bland, but not tasteless, which is why it marries so well with herbs, olives and tomatoes.

When he started making mozzarella, Mike had never tried it before. He had no idea of how it should turn out. Horace may say that he would never go through the pangs of learning again, especially the part when whole batches were thrown away, but he is happy to nibble a piece of the pliable curd in the dairy while he is busy. Even by stretching the imagination *alla pasta filata*, it's hard to believe that this foreign kickshaw could find a home in the Devon landscape, but it has. Mike's herd grows, as does the demand for his cheese.

The only ones he has to convince as to its quality are his two children. Since both are still too young to go to school they have time.

175

Part Two
the gazetteer

> Cheese is made from cow's, sheep's, goat's or buffalo milk.
>
> Milk that has not been heat-treated is maked UNP (unpasteurised) to distinguish it from P (pasteurised).
>
> Vegetarian rennet, V, used to curdle milk is suitable for vegetarians.
>
> Cheese made from organic milk is marked O.

Alham Wood Cheeses

Frances Wood pioneered buffalo farming in England, travelling to Romanian Transylvania to buy her stock. She makes cheese that's loosely based on the Central European Telemea.

Cheeses: Buffalo

P, O, V

Iambors: fresh, white, smooth, quite creamy, moist young cheese; best after four to twenty-one days.

Little Iambors in a Coat: the same Iambors cheese but allowed to develop into a soft mould-ripened cheese; best after twenty-eight to forty-two days.

Iambors with cumin: as above but with cumin, from a Romanian cheese; creamy, spreadable in a wax coating.

U, O, V

Junas: semi-hard cheese, white, firm, smooth, medium flavour and occasionally developing a dense creamy texture. Junas is sometimes sold older when it can look disturbing but has a stronger flavour.

Key suppliers: *Saturday and Sunday markets in London including Blackheath, Brentford, Broadway, Chiswick, Dulwich, Ealing, Islington, Notting Hill Pimlico, Twickenham, etc.*

Higher Alham Farm, West Cranmore, Shepton Mallet, Somerset BA4 6DD   01749 880221

Alvis Bros Ltd – Lye Cross

Started as a small farmhouse cheesemaker over half a century ago, Alvis produces about 2,500 tonnes of Cheddar a year, two-thirds of it organic. Whey from the cheesemaking feeds the 35,000 bacon pigs reared each year as part of an integrated farming system: grass – cows – milk – cheese – whey – pigs manure – grass.

Cheeses: Cow

P, O, and V (unorganic)

Cheddar: various stages of maturity (from mild to 'vintage') are sold either as Lye Cross Farmhouse or Lye Cross Organic. The differences between them? In summer, when the cattle are all on grass, it would be hard to tell the cheeses made from them apart. In winter, the organic cattle are fed silage, which gives the cheese a more milky taste, whereas the commercial cattle, kept indoors, are fed concentrates. The Lye Cross PDO Cheddar only comes from the farm's own, non-organic herd. Only cheeses nine months old or more may be sold with the PDO endorsement. Small quantities of organic territorials: Farmhouse Double Gloucester, Farmhouse Red Leicester.

Key suppliers: *a national brand.*

Lye Cross Farm, Redhill, North Somerset BS40 5RH
www.lyecrosscheese.co.uk   01934 864600

Ashley Chase Estates (Parks Farm)

Several farms on this Dorset estate (supplemented by others outside it) provide milk for about 2,000 tonnes of cheese per year. Two-thirds of this is made into traditional rounds that are sold as PDO. Its cheese is sold under the Ford Farm label by Marks & Spencer.

Cheeses: Cow

P V, some O

Some territorials: Double Gloucester, Red Leicester,

Sage Derby.

Key suppliers: *supermarkets under their own label.*

Parks Farm, Litton Cheney, Dorchester Dorset
DT2 9AZ   01308 482580

Email: mike@fordfarm.com

or ashleychase@farmhousecheesemakers.com

Ashmore Farmhouse Cheese

Pat and David Doble have made cheese on four farms in a twenty-year cheesemaking career, but they have always stuck to their principles of using single-herd milk and no pasteurisation. Their current dairy is on Lord Salisbury's estate.

Cheeses: Cow

U, V

Ashmore: the hard cheese, off-white, quite moist, has a pleasant light acidity with a clean, lactic taste; best after four to five months.

Tillingbourne: semi-soft, brined semi-soft, similar to a 'tomme' – only made intermittently.

Key suppliers: *Cranborne Chase shop; markets at Winchester, Petersfield, Southsea, Andover, Hythe.*

Lime Tree Cottage, Green Lane, Ashmore, Salisbury, Wiltshire SP5 5AQ   01747 812337

Email: david.doble@btopenworld.com

F. A. W. Baker's Kingston Farms

The Baker family has been making Cheddar since 1966. Their Somerset farm near Crewkerne has doubled in size to 1,500 acres and it has about 1,000 of its own cows being milked for cheese five days a week.

Cheeses: Cow

P, V

Cheddar: batches of 60 20kg block cheeses are packed inside wooden 'Kingston Kasks' before being sent as PDO Cheddar to supermarket clients at 12 months.

Leaze Farm, Hazelbury Plucknett, Crewkerne, Somerset TA18 7RJ   01460 72893

Email: kingston@farmhousecheesemakers.com

A.J. & R.G. Barber Ltd

This family firm has one of the longest continuous histories of cheesemaking of any English Cheddar maker. It was, for a short while after World War II, the most important supplier of Caerphilly to the Welsh mining communities. Nowadays it produces significant amounts of PDO block Cheddar. It helped to preserve and uses the same starter cultures as the Presidium Cheddar makers use.

Cheeses: Cow

P

Maryland block Cheddar: mild, mature and vintage.

Maryland vegetarian Cheddar.

Haystack block Cheddar: mild, mature and tasty.

Territorials: Wensleydale, White Cheshire, Lancashire, Caerphilly.

Most cheeses are made as smaller truckles.

Other cheeses produced: Gouda, Edam.

Key suppliers: *supermarkets.*

Onsite farm shop: Maryland Farm, Ditcheat, Shepton Mallet, Somerset, BA4 6PR

www.marylandfarm.co.uk   01749 860666

Bath Soft Cheese Co.

Graham Padfield has revived one of the few mould-ripened soft cheeses that were once made in England. It's actually not too different from Brie in texture. He has also created Wyfe of Bath a semi-soft (semi-hard?) cheese shaped a little like a curling stone, using milk from his own herd.

Cheeses: Cow

P*, O, V

* Technically 'thermised' rather than pasteurised.

Bath Soft Cheese: square, mould-ripened cheese, lightly flavoured when just ripe, but developing more character.

Wyfe of Bath: made in a basket mould, this semi-soft Gouda cheese evokes 'buttercups and water-meadows'; four months old.

Kelston Park: round Brie-type cheese.

Bath Blue: crumbly blue.

Bath Triple Crème: sometimes available.

Key suppliers: *Bath Fine Cheese Co. Paxton & Whitfield,*

Bath Fine Cheese Co., Park Farm, Kelston, Bath, Avon BA1 9AG   01225 331601
www.parkfarm.co.uk

Birdwood Farmhouse Cheesmakers

Johnathan and Melissa Ravenhill moved her farm from the Forest of Dean to the Cotswolds in 2005. Her herd, increasingly, is being switched from Friesian to dairy Shorthorn cattle that produce a rich milk similar to Ayrshire cattle.

Cheeses: Cow

U, V

Double Gloucester: traditional cloth-bound cheese, slightly heavier (4–5kg) than some; from four months old, but best at six to seven months.

Forester: hard Cheddar-style cheese but with more moisture in it; matures at a younger age, four to six months.

Dunlop: classic Scottish hard cheese.

Forest Oak: oak-smoked version of Forester.

Blue Heaven: a mould-ripened blue, like a blue Brie.

Key suppliers: *markets at Gloucester, Stroud, Cheltenham, Cirencester.*

Woefuldane Farm, Minchinhampton, Stroud, Gloucestershire GL6 9AT   01453 887065

Blissful Buffalo

Mike Hargreave's Mozzarella, made with the help of his father Horace at the western edge of Devon, took about four years' hard work, trial and error, before it reached the level of consistency it now achieves. The buffaloes are lucky in having access in summer to water-meadows and marshes for grazing.

Cheeses: Buffalo

U, V

Mozzarella: the handmade buffalo milk cheese, made to a *pasta filata*, stretched curd recipe, has a clean, milky taste and a supple texture. Vac-packed, it has a shelf-life of around a month.

Key suppliers: *markets at Tavistock, Crediton.*

Belland Farm, Tetcott, Holsworthy, Devon EX22 6RG
01409 271406

Brue Valley Farms

The Clapp family has been farming in Somerset since the sixteenth century. More recently, almost 100 years ago, it switched from cider to cheesemaking. It makes exclusively block cheese now, but using similar methods to cloth-bound rounds in order to remain within PDO rules. It's a member of the West Country Farmhouse Cheesemakers consortium, set up to promote regionally produced Cheddar.

Cheeses: Cow

P, V

Cheddar: the Clapps only make one cheese, no organic, no smoked, no special variants. It's the same whether it goes to Waitrose or Marks & Spencer; ten to sixteen months old, it's all PDO.

Key suppliers: *supermarkets.*

West Town House, Baltonsborough, Glastonbury, Somerset, BA6 8RH   01458 850260
www.brue-valley.co.uk

BV Dairy

This Dorset food company's (originally, Blackmore Vale Dairy) soft cheeses don't directly end up on the deli counter, but they are bought in large quantities by food manufacturers, in everything from cheesecakes to sandwiches.

Cheeses: Cow

P, V

Soft cheeses: they have varying fat content – 46 per cent, 30 per cent, 12 per cent, 7 per cent.
Fromage frais.
Mascarpone 38 per cent fat.

Wincombe Lane, Shaftsbury, Dorset SP7 8QD
www.bvdairy.co.uk   01747 851855

Cerney

This Cotswold dairy started by Lady Angus twenty years ago, is now managed by her daughter Barbara. Originally, it had its own goat herd, but like many others it has switched to buying in milk. The Angus family which lives in a mansion a few hundred yards from the dairy has a beautiful country garden, Cerney House Gardens, open to the public where the cheese can be sampled, together with some homemade preserves.

Cheeses: Goat

U, V

Cerney Pyramid: 200g, ash-coated Pyramid, made and sold as a fresh cheese, a Supreme Champion at the 2001 Cheese Awards.
Cerney Pepper: 120g offshoot of the Pyramid, rolled in mignonette pepper.
Starter: 50g rounds of fresh goats' cheese, similar to 'Petit Suisse'.
Cerney Banon: 140g, not always available, this slightly matured goats' cheese wrapped in vine leaves was created by Marion Conisbee-Smith (q.v.) when she was the cheesemaker here.

Key suppliers: *various delicatessens across the UK.*

Chapel Farm, North Cerney, Cirencester, Gloucestershire GL7 7DE   01285 831312
www.cerneycheese.com

Charles Martell & Son

A pioneer of the Modern British Cheese movement, since 1972, and a staunch defender of traditional Gloucester cheeses, Charles Martell uses unpasteurised milk from his herd of Gloucester cattle to make single and double, but pasteurises the bought-in

Friesian milk for his own washed rind Stinking Bishop, named after a perry pear.

Cheeses: Cow

P and U, V

Single Gloucester: natural rind, milky, young but hard cheese made with a mixture of whole and skimmed milk. It's less crumbly than some describe it, aged about 2 months; 3–4kg wheel.

Double Gloucester: natural rind, bright orange (annatto dye has been used since the seventeenth century) hard cheese, shaped as a large 3–4kg wheel, made from whole raw milk. Compact, a more silky texture than Cheddar; aged about 6 months.

Stinking Bishop: washed rind cheese (washed in perry), it has a strong cheesy smell, but the taste is milder, fruity and pleasant. It's intended to be quite runny when ripe, shaped as 2kg, flat wheel.

Slap Ma' Girdle: named after a cider apple, it's actually a fresh, nettle-wrapped cheese, only sometimes available. A joke at the expense of Cornish Yarg?

Double Berkeley: historically, this cheese was synonymous with Double Gloucester; sometimes available.

May Hill Green: a mellow semi-soft cheese flecked with nettles, sometimes available.

Key suppliers: *Neal's Yard Dairy for Stinking Bishop, all cheeses widely sold through delicatessens.*

Laurel Farm, Dymock, Gloucestershire GL18 2DP
Email: charlesmartell@lineone.net   01531 890637

Cheddar Gorge Cheese Company

Taken in hand by an ex-executive of a large dairy company, the cheesery doubles as a tourist attraction in the village of Cheddar, competing with its famous caves. It makes traditional rounds with milk from a single herd. It charges for guided visits during the summer, but in winter any-one can watch the cheese being handmade for free.

Cheeses: Cow, Sheep

U

Cheddar: the traditionals (27kg, 1.7kg truckles) matured on site, have an open texture and a relatively sweet, nutty taste.

Oak smoked Cheddar: cheeses are pre-cut, smoked and vacuum packed.

Cheddar with wild garlic and herbs: the flavourings are added, fresh to the vat at the same time as the salt is added and the cheese is matured for five months rather than a year with the standard cheese.

Cheddar with cider, garlic and chives (made as above).

Cheddar with a slosh of port: the port is mixed with the milled curd at the same time as the salt is added. It's apparent as veined streaks in the finished cheese.

Cheddar with chilli and a touch of paprika (made as above).

The Cliffs, Cheddar Gorge, Somerset BS27 3QA
01934 742810
www.cheddargorgecheeseco.co.uk

Conisbee Traditionals

Marion Conisbee-Smith used to be the Cerney cheesemaker (q.v.). She has researched historic cheeses to make from her small herd of Gloucester cattle. She is in the process of setting up a dairy and aims to make cheese commercially again in 2007.

Cheeses: Cow

U, V

Pineapple: the 4-month old, 3–4kg cheese is hung from a net to mature. The name reflects the shape.

Finchback: this fresh Gloucester-milk cheese weighs about 1kg, is shaped like Brie and wrapped in raspberry leaves.

Key suppliers: *Bath Fine Cheese Co*

Parsons Cottage, George Street, Bisley, Stroud GL6 7BB   01452 770915

Cornish Cheese Company

Making a Dolcelatte, softish blue cheese, has proved to be an instant success for Philip Stansfield. Coming down to Cornwall from Cheshire to establish a dairy farm, he decided to become a cheesemaker when the fall in milk prices threatened his livelihood. He took a course at Chris Ashby's AB Cheesemaking school near Nottingham before returning to make Cornish Blue. Early experiments with Tinner's Blue and a cheese called Beast of Bodmin have been shelved to concentrate on one that is already available nationally and can rival the famous Italian formaggi.

Cheeses: Cow

P, V

Cornish Blue: The softish blue is made in a range of sizes from 5kg down to 500g. Ready to eat between twelve and fourteen weeks, it has a spreadable texture that never becomes runny.

Key suppliers: *Available at farm shop and across the UK.*

Knowle Farm, Upton Cross, Liskeard, Cornwall
PL14 5BG   01579 363660
www.cornishcheese.co.uk

Cornish Country Larder

John Gaylard, a goat farmer turned cheesemaker, has sister factories in Somerset and North Cornwall. In the Duchy, he produces his St Endelion brand, that has become one of the most popular High Street Bries, probably because its very high fat content gives it an extra rich texture. His goats' cheeses, he made his first in 1984, are also being produced by the tonne nowadays and sold by multiple retailers.

Cheeses: Cow, Goat

P, V, some O

Cows' milk:

Cornish Brie and organic Cornish Brie: available either in a chunky 3kg wheel or a smaller 1kg one.
St Endelion: made as a 1kg wheel to a standard mould-ripened Brie formula with the addition of Cornish double cream.
Chatel: in 200g rounds, it's very similar to St Endelion, a touch less rich, made to compete with commercial Camemberts in size but to a Brie recipe.
Farmhouse Cheddar: block cheeses, ten to twelve months old.

Goats' milk:

Gevrik: a small mould-ripened goats' cheese that's rich in fat (26 per cent) and becomes runny when aged; 70g cylinders.
St Anthony's: a rich, brined, mould-ripened cheese in a rectangular log shape — aged for eight weeks.
Goats' Cheddar: Six-month-old block Cheddar.
Village Green: Waxed, six-month-old hard goats' cheese.

Key suppliers: *St Endelion is a brand sold across the UK.*

The Creamery, Trevarrian, Newquay, Cornwall
TR8 4AH   01637 860331
North Bradon Farm, Isle Abbotts, Taunton, Somerset TA3 6RY   01460 281688
www.ccl-ltd.co.uk

Cornish Farmhouse Cheeses

Caryl Minson was one of the first Cornish cheesemakers and her farm shop at Menallack specialises in the county's cheeses – approaching 50 assorted kinds. She produces her own – up to nineteen varieties – at any time from cows', sheep's, goats' and buffaloes' milk. The hards are unpasteurised and the softs derived from pasteurised milk.

Cheeses: Cow, Sheep, Goat, Buffalo

P, U, V

Cows' milk

Menallack Farmhouse: unpasteurised cows' milk cheese made to a Cheshire cheese recipe, 2.5kg and 5kg.

Menallack Chives and Garlic: same cheese as the above but with herb/onion layers.

St Erme

St Lauda: a hard blue cheese, like certain gorgonzolas before they go creamy.

Goats' milk

Cornish Herb Whirl

Fingal

Polmesk

Vithen

Sheep's milk

Cheetham's Chough

Nanterrow: a recipe inherited from a cheesemaking St Ives doctor, it's a rich, smooth, fresh cheese.

Nanterrow Herb and Garlic

Tala: five-month-old hard cheese with a 48 per cent butter fat content. Also sometimes smoked.

Buffalo milk

Blissful Buffalo: soft.

Mixed milk

Heligan: first made for Tim Schmidt when he opened the Lost Gardens of Heligan, before the Eden Project. It's a soft mixed-milk cheese with lemon zests.

Mrs Finn: a plain fresh, cow/sheep cheese.

Treverva Green: fresh cow/sheep cheese with green peppercorns.

Key suppliers: *direct sale from the farm shop.*

Menallack Farm, Treverva, Penryn, Cornwall TR10 9BP   01326 340333
Email: menallack@fsbdial.co.uk

Country Cheeses

Although not strictly a cheesemaker this shop, run by Elise and Gary Jugheim, has a number of cheeses, mainly seasonal, made exclusively for it.

Cheeses: Cow, Goat

Trehill: a smooth cows'-milk cheese made to a Curworthy recipe by Rachel Stevens, flavoured with garlic, 2kg.

Devon Sage: made by Rachel Stevens (above), with sage flavouring, 2kg.

Sweet Charlotte: made by Rachel Stevens, waxy Emmenthal-type cheese, aged up to six months.

Blue Hills: unpasterised, a rich spreadable blue made from a mixture of Jersey and goats' milk, 1kg.

Celeste: made at Sharpham, a runny Camembert-type cheese made from Jersey milk, 200g.

Bakesey Meadow: made at Sharpham, mould-ripened, goats' milk, best at six–eight weeks, 170g.

Withy Brook: made at Sharpham, an ash-coated pyramid.

Market Road, Tavistock,
Devon PL19 0BW   01822 615035
26 Fore Street, Topsham,
Devon EX3 0HD   01392 877746
www.countrycheeses.co.uk

Cranborne Chase Cheese

Richard Biddlecombe was one of the first graduates of Chris Ashby's, AB Cheesemaking school. A farm manager on an estate near Salisbury, he took the course together with the owner, Peter Kininmouth. Soon after their return to the West Country, the herd was sold, but Richard continued on his new career as a cheesemaker. He produces soft and semi-soft cheeses with milk from a single herd, the same supplier used by Ashmore cheese.

Cheeses: Cow

U, some V

Win Green: An unpasteurised, mould-ripened cheese, it gains from being made with raw milk. The appearance of the dusty white and milky coffee-coloured rind is distinct from many other English soft cheeses. The texture is dense like clotted cream and the flavour comparable to a Normandy Camembert, 250g approx.

St Nicholas: This small lactic-curd (made without rennet) cheese has a lemony taste when young and a texture like under-ripe Camembert. As it ages the texture grows smoother to become virtually spreadable, 150g.

Alderwood: One of the larger washed-rind cheeses, its springy curd has a pale straw colour, that's dappled with tiny holes, 2kg. The flavour is unmistakeably fruity. It can be eaten at any stage between three and five months.

Key suppliers: *delicatessans and restaurants through wholesaler: Longman Cheese Sales*

Estate Office, Manor Farm, Ashmore,
Salisbury, Wiltshire SP5 5AE   01747 811125
www.cranbornechasecheese.co.uk

Cricketer Farm

The farm was started by the late Lord Beaverbrook in the 1940s. It makes traditional and block Cheddar, but mainly half-fat cheeses with milk collected from twenty-five farms in the vicinity of Nether Stowey, near the Bristol Channel.

Cheeses: Cow

P, V

Farmhouse and traditional Cheddar: this is made both as a traditional cloth-bound cheese and block Cheddar. It was champion cheese at the Bath & West Show in 2005.

'Half-fat' cheese: available both as a white and a red annatto-dyed block cheese.

Quantock Gold: made with Channel Island milk, it has a smoother texture than conventional Cheddars.

Goats' Cheese: Four months and over hard cheese.

Own farm shop and tearooms where the cheeses can be sampled. This national brand is also available across the UK.

Stowey Court Farm, Nether Stowey, Bridgwater, Somerset TA5 1LL
Farm shop: 01278 732 207 Office: 01278 732084
www.cricketerfarm.co.uk

Curworthy Cheese

One of the first Modern British cheeses, Curworthy was developed on a farm managed by the magazine *Farmer's Weekly*. Rachel Stevens first made it there, then in her own dairy. The cheese is made to a scalded-curd recipe, based on a very early English cheese, but different stages of maturity change its character.

Cheeses: Cow

P, V, and non-V

Curworthy: somewhere between semi-hard and hard, Curworthy has a compact creamy texture and a mild flavour that's light on acidity, tasting of best milk. It's sold waxed, but matured as medium-sized rounds, 1–1.3kg).

Devon Oke: the aged version is made as a larger wheel, using the standard Curworthy recipe. At about eight months old it develops a richer rounder flavour.

Belstone: the same as Curworthy, but made with vegetarian rennet.

Meldon, and Chipple and Vergin: three similar flavoured cheeses in which flavours are mixed in with the curd during making. Meldon, for instance, tastes of mustard and ale.

Key suppliers: *Country Cheeses, Bath Fine Cheese Co.*

Stockbeare Farm, Jacobstowe, Okehampton, Devon EX20 3PZ   01837 810587
www.curworthycheese.co.uk

Dairy Crest

The Davidstow creamery in North Cornwall is the largest cheesemaking factory in the country producing around 55,000 tonnes of cheese in a year with milk from 500 farms. To give an idea of the scale, that's over 1,000 times more than most specialist cheesemakers.

Cathedral City: This is the largest-selling branded cheese in the country, sold as 'mature yet mellow'. It represents the culmination of over 150 years of international experience in industrial-scale cheese-making technology.

Davidstow: Cornish block Cheddar.

Key suppliers: *a massive national brand sold across the UK.*

Dairy Crest, Davidstow, Camelford, Cornwall PL32 9XW   01840261322
www.dairycrest.co.uk

Daisy and Co.

The most exciting thing about the three cheeses produced on an organic farm at the edge of the Mendip Hills are their names, taken from members of the Daisy family.

Cheeses: Cow

P, V, O

Goldilocks: the mould-ripened, Camembert-style cheese is made from Channel Island milk. It has a buttery texture and very mild taste under a white, thickish crust. It's also available as an oak-smoked product.

Black Eyed Susan: the same cheese as Goldilocks, but coated with cracked peppercorns.

Corn Marigold: a young, hard cheese in the Cheddar family, the company describes it as 'popular with children'.

Key suppliers: *Longman's (q.v.)*

Tree Tops Farm, North Brewham, Bruton, Somerset BA10 0JS   01749 850254
www.daisyandco.co.uk

Daylesford Creamery

Daylesford has been a successful attempt at creating a new Rolls Royce cheese.

Cheeses: Cow

U, V, O

Daylesford: made a little larger than a Cheddar truckle and the texture, a touch moister than many aged farmhouse Cheddars, is almost sliceable. The flavour, though, is rich, round and complex, starting from the rind and working its way into the heart of the cheese. Best at about eight months.

Penystone: mould-ripened or washed-rind organic cheese, it's shaped like a flat brick and has been made both ways, 300g. The taste is milder than some matured soft cheeses and it doesn't smell as strong as others.

Key suppliers: *own shop and Neal's Yard Dairy.*

New Farm, Daylesford, Moreton-in-Marsh,

Gloucestershire GL56 0YG   01608 731700
www.daylesfordorganic.com

Denhay Farms Ltd

George and Amanda Streatfield have five herds of dairy cows from which they produce cheese. Until recently the whey from the making fed pigs that were converted into some of the best bacon and air-dried hams in the country. They still produce these, but have abandoned pig farming.

Cheeses: Cow

P

Cheddar: aged Cheddar is made traditionally in bandaged rounds (27kg) or in boxes (20kg) to produce mature PDO cheeses.

Dorset Drum: The 2kg truckles of Cheddar are aged from six to nine months.

Oak-smoked Cheddar: mature cheese smoked in 200g pieces.

Key suppliers: *supermarkets.*

Broadoak, Bridport, Dorset DT6 5NP
www.denhay.co.uk   01308 458963

Dorset Blue Vinny Cheese

Mike Davies is the reviver and sole maker of Dorset Blue Cheese. Once a farmhouse cheese that blued naturally, if intermittently, it disappeared from Dorset farms until he began making it on his farm in the 1980s.

Cheeses: Cow

V, U

Dorset Blue Vinny: the cheese was traditionally made from skimmed milk, a recipe that Mike inititially copied. He has since adjusted the recipe so it's a little less crumbly than it once was. The veining, a flecked tracery of blue, looks quite different from Stilton. The taste is similar, though the single-herd milk gives it a distinct personality.

Key suppliers: *delicatessens.*

Woodbridge Farm, Stock Gaylard, Sturminster Newton, Dorset DT10 2BD   01963 23133
www.dorsetblue.com

R. A. Duckett and Co.

Chris Duckett is an expert Caerphilly maker who moved his dairy from his farm on the Somerset Levels into the Mendips. He shares space with the Cheddar maker, Westcombe Dairy. His cheeses are generally eaten young, but those sent to Neal's Yard Dairy in London are aged until they develop a hard rind. By then the cheese has altered in character, becoming more creamy in texture, with a round mouth-filling taste.

Cheeses: Cow

P, some U, V

Caerphilly: the cheese has the traditional character of a miner's cheese. It's moist, open textured without being over crumbly and has a thirst-quenching acidity.
Wedmore and Smoked Wedmore: the compact semi-soft cheeses flavoured with herbs make an unusual, but interesting toasting cheese.

Key suppliers: *Neal's Yard Dairy.*

Walnut Tree Farm, Heath House, Wedmore, Somerset BS28 4UJ   01934 712218
Email: walnuttreefarm@zoom.co.uk

Exmoor Blue Cheese

This long-standing craft cheesemaker, started on a farm (now no longer) has always made quite young, relatively small, relatively mild, unpasteurised, mainly blue cheeses.

Cheeses: Cow, Sheep, Goat, Buffalo

U, V

Exmoor Jersey Blue (PGI): the company's signature cheese, made from Jersey milk, is similar in style to Dolcelatte. Its texture can be quite firm or Brie-like, depending on the season. Best from six weeks old, 1.2kg approx.

Partridges Blue: another cows'-milk blue, a little smaller and a little more compact in texture, a more concentrated flavour. Best from six weeks old, 1.2kg approx.

Somerset Blue: a harder, more crumbly blue that has been hand-milled and hand-pressed after draining the whey. Best from six to eight weeks, 2.5kg approx. drum.

Brendon Blue: quite mild goats' cheese with blue veining. Smaller than Beenleigh Blue with which it has similarities. Best from six weeks, 1kg drum.

Baby Brendon: semi-fresh (twenty-eight days old) white goats' cheese, 500g.

Goat's cheese with herbs in oil.

Quantock Blue: stronger flavoured, rich, sheep's-milk cheese. Best from six to eight weeks, 1kg drum.

Blissful Buffalo Blue: the most creamy texture blue cheese in the Exmoor stable. Best from six to eight weeks, 1kg drum.

Key suppliers: *available through delicatessens.*

Willett Farm, Lydeard St Lawrence, Taunton, Somerset TA4 3QB   01984 667328
Email: exmoorbluecheese@btopenworld.com

Godminster Vintage

Godminster is a large organic farm that began cheesemaking in 1999. Farmer Richard Holingbery has described his herd of 200 cows as 'athletes' in training for a daily milking Olympics. To keep them fit and healthy he has resorted to acupuncture, massage and peppermint-oil treatments. This is new cool farming and cool cheese to match.

Cheeses: Cow

P, V, O

Cheddar: Godminster has its own take on Cheddar making. The block cheese is matured for a year, extruded to give it a softer, creamier texture than conventional Cheddar and then waxed in various sizes from 400g to 2kg.

Key suppliers: *this is a fashionable brand that is generally available in delicatessens and food stores.*

Godminster Farm, Bruton, Somerset BA10 0NE
www.godminster.com   01749 813733

Godsell's Church Farm Cheese

Elizabeth Godsell studied cheese, yoghurt and ice-cream making at Cannington College near Bridgwater, before adding a cheesery to her 500-acre dairy farm. She was planning on calling her first hard cheese 'Black Bitch', but was advised that the name was politically incorrect. Instead, it became Leonard Stanley, named after the village where she lives.

Cheeses: Cow

P, V

Leonard Stanley: a hard cheese of Cheddar type made either with a natural rind or a dark green waxed one, 4kg approx., stored for a minimum seven months.

Single Gloucester: the traditional skimmed-milk cheese is made in the same moulds as the Leonard Stanley rather than wheels.

Smoked Single Gloucester: Elizabeth Godsell quarters the cheese and smokes the pieces using oak chippings.

Double Gloucester: the classic hard, annatto-coloured cheese, made from whole milk, is aged for at least five months before it's sold.

Nympsfield: this fresh, ball-shaped cheese (150g) eaten under two weeks old is transformed into Scary Mary.

Scary Mary: after about twelve weeks affinage, natural moulds form on the surface and it develops a Brie-like, almost runny, yellow curd. Don't try to eat the outer mould!

Key suppliers: *farmers' markets at Nailsworth, Stroud.*

Dougall's, Church Road, Leonard Stanley, Stonehouse, Gloucestershire GL10 3NP   01453 827802

Email: godsellscheese@btinternet.com

Gould, E. F. J. and Co.

The family has farmed on the Pennard Ridge near Glastonbury for seventy years and been making large rounds for forty. When he was eleven, farmer Fred Gould made his first cheese for his father, who started the dairy, and his sister Jean is the current cheesemaker in chief.

Cheeses: Cow

P

Cheddar: only half-hundredweight PDO rounds of cheese are made on the farm together with 2kg truckles.

Key suppliers: *this is a big farmhouse brand sold in multiples.*

Batch Farm, East Pennard, Shepton Mallet, Somerset BA4 6TU   01749 860319

Email: efjgould@farmhousecheesemakers.com

Greens of Glastonbury

Making cheese since the 1920s Green's is, year in year out, one of the star Cheddar makers. It started producing organic cheese in 2003 and in 2006 won the *Daily Telegraph-*Sainsbury prize for the best organic product of the year. Milk comes from the farm's herd on the Somerset Levels.

Cheeses: Cow

P, O, non-O

Cheddar: the nine-month-old minimum PDO cheese, made in traditional rounds is made in both organic and non-organic versions. Most of the cheese is snapped up by the supermarket buyers.

Double Gloucester: aged for between six and nine months, the cheeses are made much larger than traditional Gloucesters, but have the characteristic citric tang and buttery texture.

Key suppliers: *Waitrose through West Country Farhouse Cheesemakers*

Redlake Dairy, Newtown Farm, Page Lane, West Pennard, Glastonbury, Somerset BA5 2DF
          01458 834414

Email: greens@farmhousecheesemakers.com

Ilchester Cheese Co. Ltd

Something of an institution, Ilchester Cheese supplies multiples across the land with mango and ginger flavoured cheese, or any among hundreds of flavoured varieties. It doesn't make any cheese itself but buys Cheddar and other territorials from Barber's at different levels of maturity from three months to a year, grates it and, under pressure, compacts it with the chosen flavour. It's Britain's largest cheese exporter – not a lot of people know that. The company started in 1962 when hotel owner Ken Seaton mixed grated cheese with a once-famous beer, Worthington E, and added some powdered spices. He packed the mixture in cartons and sold them for four shillings and sixpence the half pound.

Cheeses: Cow

P, V

Mexicana: typical of the Ilchester approach, a young Cheddar is shredded and then blended with bell, jalapeño and chilli peppers. The cheeses are hand rolled in spices too.

Original Beer Cheese: this black-waxed cheese, made to the original recipe, except that the beer is now supplied by Fullers, is quite hard to track down and made as special batches or for special clients.

Key suppliers: *most flavoured Ilchester cheeses are sold on deli counters in multiples; if it's labelled 'strawberry and elderflower' then it's probably been made by the company, which tests ten to fifteen new recipes each month.*

Somerton Road, Ilchester, Somerset BA22 8JL
www.ilchester.co.uk   01935 842800

Keen's Cheddar Ltd

'Cheese has been made by the Keens at Moorhayes Farm since our Great Aunt Jane pressed her first truckle in 1899. Our mother Dorothy learnt cheesemaking at the Somerset Farm Institute in Cannington. Nowadays, me and my brother Stephen, assisted by our sons Nick and James, continue to make unpasteurised Cheddar – we're one of only a few farms who do.' George Keen.

Cheeses: Cow

U

Cheddar: Cheddar from Keen's, along with Montgomery's and Westcombe's make up the highly valued Presidium cheese consortium established by the Slow Food movement. It uses traditional starters and rennets as well as raw milk. It is sweeter than Montgomery's, but has the characteristic nutty flavour that Cheddar connoisseurs admire.

Key suppliers: *Neal's Yard Dairy, Bath Fine Cheese Co., Country Cheeses and specialist cheese shops.*

Moorhayes Farm, Verrington Lane, Wincanton, Somerset BA9 8JR   01963 32286
www.keenscheddar.co.uk

Loddiswell Cheese

Loddiswell started out as a goats' cheese. In 1994 it won a major prize at the Cheese Awards. That year the South Hams farm where it was made was burnt down by an arsonist and the goats killed. Eight years later, dairy farmer Roger Grudge bought the name, switched to making cows'-milk cheese with his herd of Swiss Brown cattle near Kingsbridge, selling cheese 'Fresh from the Devon Alps'. Two years later he moved to Oxford, but he is returning to make cheese three days a week at Stokeley Farm, which has its own farm shop in a new dairy. The characteristic of all Loddiswell cheeses is that they are extra low in salt.

Cheeses: Cow, Goat

P, V, some O

Aveton: this goats' cheese links to the original maker of Loddiswell, Jocelyn Martin. It's a semi-hard cheese matured for eight to ten weeks, weighing about 3.5kg.

Hazelwood: the cows'-milk cheese, similar in texture to Alpine washed-rind cheeses, it is brine-washed and matured for ten to fourteen weeks, weighing about 3.5kg.

Old Lodd: the curd is heated and the whey washed out of it to produce a buttery cheese that ripens at around five months; available in winter.

Moreleigh: the brother of Old Lodd its produced from winter milk; available in summer.

Key suppliers: *farm shop and local delicatessens.*

Stokeley Farm Shop, Stokeley Barton, Stokenham, Kingsbridge, Devon TQ7 2SE   01548 581010

J.K. Longman (Longman's Cheese Sales)

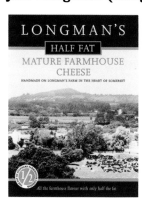

This large family dairy farm near Yeovil – 1,000 hectares, 1,000 cows – has grown into a large supplier of reduced-fat Cheddar. It's usually aged between ten and fourteen months, not less than eight. Made with semi-skimmed milk, it has half the fat content (16 per cent) of other Cheddars. It's a company that also sells and distributes artisan cheeses for small-scale cheesemakers.

Cheeses: Cow

P, V

Longman Light: A medium-fat, extra-mature cheese which retains a good taste although the fat content has been reduced by half, from 34 per cent to 16 per cent.

Longman Matureman: a well-rounded mature Cheddar cheese of at least ten months of age.

Longman Strongman: a farmhouse Cheddar with a distinctive extra-mature old-fashioned flavour.

Longman Vintage XXX: an eighteen-month-old vintage block farmhouse Cheddar. A great cheese with a real bite to it.

Longman Youngman: the creamy mild-medium flavoured cheese aged between four and six months.

Key suppliers: *national sales through multiples and delicatessens.*

Fir Tree, Galhampton, Yeovil, Somerset BA22 7BH
www.longman-cheese-sales.co.uk   01963 441146

Loosehanger Farmhouse Cheeses LLP

Using milk from a pedigree Ayrshire herd, this small dairy produces washed-curd cheeses loosely derived from Dutch and Belgian techniques and creamy blues.

Cheeses: Cow

P, V

Woodfall's Oak: this washed-curd cheese of 3–4kg made in Gouda moulds is mild-flavoured with a silky supple texture, pocked with small holes. It's made to be eaten young, around eight weeks and is also made with flavourings added.

Woodfall's Stromboli: as above, but with added sun-dried tomatoes and basil.

Woodfall's Bustard with Mustard: horseradish, mustard and Bustard beer are added to the curds in the vat to give a gentle, rather than assertive, seasoning.

Hampshire Rose: the same cheese as Woodfall's

Oak, it's aged six months to give it more body, a firmer texture and extra flavour.

Old Sarum: this creamy blue cheese is made as a small truckle rather than a stilton size.

New Forest: a second blue cheese produced with a different blueing agent to Old Sarum.

Key suppliers: *farm shop.*

Home Farm, Whiteshoot, Redlynch, Salisbury, Wiltshire SP5 2PR   01725 514791

www.cheeseproducer.com

Lubborn Creamery

Pioneering large-scale production of Brie and mould-ripened goats' cheese in Britain. Lubborn created two rivals to what had previously been available only as French imports.

Cheeses: Cow, Goat

Capricorn Goats' Cheese: the white-mould cheeses can be enjoyed at different stages of ripeness. The core is hard and crumbly at first but changes to a creamy almost runny texture as it ripens. It's sold both as small cylinders and in wedges like Brie.

Somerset Brie and Somerset Organic Brie: the two cheeses are almost identical, except that the organic milk produces a cheese with a little more butter fat in it.

Key suppliers: *a national brand found across the UK.*

Manor Farm, Cricket St Thomas, Chard, Somerset TA20 4BZ   01460 30736

www.lubborn.co.uk

Lyburn Farmhouse Cheesemakers

Lyburn Farm, on the edge of the New Forest, produces organic vegetables and squashes for a major supermarket, but it also makes both pasteurised and unpasteurised cheeses that are non-organic, using milk from its own herd. Though still a small and new craft maker, it's already exporting cheeses into a chain of American wholefood stores.

Cheeses: Cow

U, P, V

Lyburn Gold: the lightly coloured 4–5kg wheels, similar in style to artisan Gouda cheese, have a smooth, buttery texture and light acidity. Made in its unpasteurised version it develops more complex flavours at about four months old. It's also available in smoked wedges and speckled with garlic and nettles.

Lyburn's Winchester: Lyburn Gold is left to mature for up to eight months during which time its texture changes from bouncy to creamy. Aged for up to fourteen months it becomes fuller flavoured, an English take on the classic Dutch Old Amsterdam cheese.

Lyburn Cumin: similar to the Dutch Gouda with cumin, it's a cheese that is often eaten for breakfast in Holland.

Key suppliers: *Lyburn goes to nineteen Hampshire and Wiltshire farmers' markets including that at Winchester.*

Lyburn Farm, Landford, Salisbury, Wiltshire SP5 2DN

www.lyburnfarm.co.uk   01794 390451

Lynher Dairies Cheese Co.

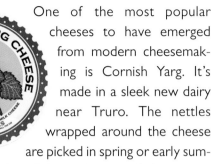

One of the most popular cheeses to have emerged from modern cheesemaking is Cornish Yarg. It's made in a sleek new dairy near Truro. The nettles wrapped around the cheese are picked in spring or early summer, frozen and used during the rest of the year.

Cheeses: Cow

P, V

Cornish Yarg: the nettle-coloured wheels weighing about 3kg produce an open-textured slightly crumbly cheese similar to Caerphilly. It's young and any taste from the nettles is virtually impossible to distinguish.
Wild Garlic Yarg: the same basic cheese wrapped in garlic leaves that do transmit their taste to the cheeses.
Cornish Garland: this cheese has moved across the border from Devon where it used to be made as Devon Garland by a craft cheesemaker who closed down. It's a pleasant hard cheese with herbs running through the middle of it.

Key suppliers: *the standard Yarg is nationally available, but an aged relative that has undergone changes to the original recipe, such as the use of animal rennet, is sold from Neal's Yard Dairy. It looks a lot less pretty but has more depth of flavour and a creamier texture.*

Ponsanooth, Truro, Cornwall TR3 7JH
www.lynherdairies.co.uk   01872 870789

Middle Campscott Farm

On a smallholding overlooking the Bristol Channel Karen and Lawrence Wright have been making small quantities of hard sheep's-milk cheese for the last thirteen years and more recently goats' cheese. The flock is only milked for cheese six months a year, but cheeses' textures vary winter to summer.

Cheeses: Sheep, Goat

U, V, O

Campscott: made as a small, 1kg truckle with a mottled rind and aged from three months onwards. In texture it's Manchego-like, though more crumbly during the summer than in winter. There are seasonal differences in taste too. The summer cheese is cleaner tasting, but in winter it's more earthy.
Campscott Goat: five goats live in the smallholding's 'Goats' Palace' so the only a few cheeses are made. They are similar in style to their sheep sisters, but are especially creamy in winter.

Key suppliers: *farmers' markets and at the farm gate.*

Middle Campscott Farm, Lee, Ilfracombe,
North Devon EX34 8LS   01271 864621
www.middlecampscott.co.uk

Miller's Cheesehouse

This recently started cheese processor is a miniature equivalent of the early days of Ilchester Cheese Co. Owned by an ex-publican, it makes spreadable, flavoured cheeses pâtés that are sold in tubs.

Cheeses: Cow

P, V

Spreads, in 70g, 500g and 1kg tubs include: Black olive, curried mango, grilled peppers, Provençal, roasted onions, sweet chillis, tomato and basil and wholegrain mustard.

Key suppliers: *sells direct to local pubs.*

17 Queen's Acre, Newnham-on-Severn,
Gloucestershire GL14 1DJ   01594 516335
jane@millerscheesehouse.co.uk

J. A. & E. Montgomery

Cheddar made on his farm near Cadbury Castle enjoys a global reputation. It's one of three Presidium Cheddars (an accolade devised by the Slow Food movement) along with Keen's and Westcombe.

Although he sticks very close to traditional Cheddar manufacture, James Montgomery's handling of his dairy herd and the milk it produces is crucial to the success of his cheeses.

Cheeses: Cow

U

Cheddar: texture and taste vary with the cheese, perhaps more than other Cheddars. This may depend in part on the age, but mainly on the make. Over eighteen months old it's a powerful, almost meaty cheese. When younger it has the classic nutty Cheddar taste. It can be hard and fatty or slightly crumbly. Very old, it can have some crystallization in the curd that's experienced as crunchy bits between the teeth.

Jersey Shield: the washed-curd cheese, matured for six or seven months is made as a large truckle from the farm's herd of Jersey cows. It's hardish and mellow with a nice balance between sweet and savoury flavours.

Ogle shield: cheese made to the Jersey Shield recipe is washed in brine (at Neal's Yard Dairy) to develop a sticky outer rind that changes the maturation of the curd.

Key suppliers: *Neal's Yard Dairy, Country Cheeses, Bath Fine Cheese Co., major food shops.*

Manor Farm, Woolston Road, North Cadbury, Yeovil, Somerset BA22 7DW   01963 440243
Email: jamie@montycheese.fsnet.co.uk

Neet Foods Ltd

Hugh Brodie runs a neat, modern, dairy outside Bude where fresh cheeses are hung to drain as in Granny's days, but the small cheese balls he produces have a Jamie Oliver chic about them that lends itself to modern cookery.

Cheeses: Cow, Goat

P, V

St Marwenne: walnut-sized balls of fresh cheese, bottled either as goats' milk or cows' milk, are packed neatly in jam jars topped up with a neutral oil and fresh herbs and garlic. The goat is the softer of the two with a pleasant tang to it.

Key suppliers: *Bath Fine Cheese Co. and delicatessens.*

Trelay Farm, Marhamchurch, Bude,
Cornwall EX32 0HB   01288 361142
Email: Hugh.brodie@ntlworld.com

Norsworthy Dairy Goats

Dave Johnson has built up a small herd of Saanen, Alpines and Toggenburg goats on his farm near Crediton. At first he supplied the likes of Robin Congdon with milk. But now, taught by a Dutch lady who was his first dairymaid, he also makes his own cheeses.

Cheeses: Goat

U, V

Norsworthy: the mild washed-curd goats' cheese (2.5kg) is made to a washed-curd recipe that gives it a springy semi-hard texture. It's eaten young at one month when it has a mild goaty taste.

Gunstone: coloured with annatto like Gloucesters, it's a little older than the Norsworthy, but similar in size and style. It can be matured to eight months when it develops a range of subtle goat flavours.

Fresh goats' cheese: hung to drain and sold within

days of making this is a perky, clean-tasting cheese.

Key suppliers: *farmers' markets at Tavistock, Exeter, Crediton, Plymouth, Kingsbridge.*

Frankland Cottage, Gunstone, Crediton, Devon
EX17 5WJ   01363 775326
Email: davejohnson@lineone.net

Olive Farm (Babcary) Ltd

For several years, David Paull has been taking his raw milk and cream from a pedigree herd of Guernsey cows to the larger markets. He has started converting some of the milk to cheese.

Cheeses: Cow
U
Caerphilly: because of the larger fat globules in Guernsey milk, the cheese is closer textured than many Caerphilly cheeses and has a yellowish colour. Cheddar: the farm is a newcomer to cheesemaking and has experimented with both rounds and blocks of cheese, but they are all made from a milk that is not normally associated with Cheddar.

Key suppliers: *markets at Islington, Notting Hill, Marylebone and Oxford, Guildford, Frome.*

Olive Farm, Babcary, Somerton, Somerset TA11 7ES
                                    01458 223229

Parkham Farms

One of the larger farmhouse cheesemakers, and the westernmost member of the PDO Cheddar scheme, Parkham manufactures about 3,000 tonnes of aged block cheese per year. Milk comes from a herd of 1,400 cows and from twenty-five neighbouring farms. Its cheeses are sold by giants Dairy Crest and North Downs Dairy.

Cheeses: Cow
P, V

Cheddar: Consistent block Cheddar cheese is made at various stages of maturity.

Key suppliers: *major supermarkets under its own name and also under Dairy Crest and Pilgrim's Choice labels.*

Higher Alminstone Farm, Woolsery, Bideford, North Devon EX39 5PX   01237 431246
www.parkhamfarms.com

Pilgrim's Choice North Downs Dairy

 This large rival to Dairy Crest buys buys its cheese from members of the West Country Farmhouse Cheesemakers and packs them as "Mature", "Vintage", "Strong" and "Reserve" to its own standards.

Cheeses: Cow
P, V
Key suppliers: *All major supermarket chains.*
S
axon Way, Wincanton Business Park, Wincanton, Somerset   01963 828828
www.pilgrimschoice.com

Quicke's Traditional Ltd

 Mary Quicke is a cheesemaker whose cheeses are sought after around the world. Her Devonshire family has been farming at Newton St Cyres near Exeter since the time of Henry VIII, but its history as a cheesemaker goes back to 1972 when her mother started maturing traditional Cheddar, using milk from her own herd. The farm is unusual in that the cattle are kept out of doors on grass for eleven months a year, which gives the Cheddars, in particular, a flavour that Randolph Hodgson of Neal's Yard Dairy describes as reminiscent of Opel Fruits.

Cheeses: Cow, Goat

P, some U

Quicke's Traditional Mature: 'Intense and tangy, with hints of almonds and hazelnuts, with a searing acidity.' It's aged upwards of nine months. The flavour has what wine connoisseurs describe as length; it stays in the mouth long after the cheese has vanished down the gullet.

Quicke's Mild: the same cheese is sold young from three to six months while it still has a pleasant fresh flavour.

Vintage Small: normally sold through the farm shop. If there's curd left in the vat, but not enough to make a whole cheese, it's made into a half (roughly 12kg) size and aged twelve to fifteen months.

Herb Cheddar: a cheese to which fresh herbs are added in the vat at the same time as the salt.

Oak-Smoked Cheddar: wedges of cheese are smoked on the farm using wood from the estate.

St Cyres: goats' Cheddar. It's drier than many hard goats' cheeses and aged for a year.

Double Gloucester: made as a large 25kg drum, 8kg and a 1.8kg cheese.

Red Leicester: lighter, moister, younger than Cheddar, it has a deep orange tinge and, at six months, a tangy, lemony taste.

Key suppliers: *own farm shop and gardens; Neal's Yard Dairy and major food stores.*

Home Farm, Newton St Cyres, Exeter,
Devon EX5 5AY   01392 851222
www.quickes.co.uk

Rosary Goats' Cheese

ROSARY GOATS CHEESE

Located a few miles outside Salisbury, Chris and Claire Moody buy goats' milk that they turn into immaculate, no-frills fresh cheeses in their pristine dairy.

Cheeses: Goat

P, V

Rosary: the burger-sized disc of fresh cheese, best up to four weeks old, has a zingy, lemony taste up front, with a subdued taste of goats' milk. The texture is open and moussy, still very moist and lightly salted.

Rosary Ash: the ash-coated Rosary is just the same as the Rosary above but with black lingerie.

Rosary Pepper: adapted from the Rosary (above), it's perhaps a little drier, fluffy with a coating of crushed black pepper that marries well with the creamy texture.

Rosary Garlic and Herb: a Gold Medal winner at the Cheese Awards, the balance of herbs and garlic with the clean-tasting cream cheese is ideal.

Key suppliers: *farmers' market at Winchester.*

The Rosary, Partridge Hill, Landford, Salisbury, Wiltshire SP5 2BB   01794 322196

Ruddle Court Cheese

Ruddle Court Farm's soft cheeses are made on the farm from the milk of their own Friesian cows, on the banks of the River Severn at Newnham.

Cheeses: Cow

P, V

Ruddle Court White: mould-ripened Camembert-style cheese.

Ruddle Court Fresh.

Key suppliers: *farmers' markets at Stow-on-the-Wold, Gloucester, Abergavenny, Stroud, Ross-on-Wye.*

Ruddle Court Farm, Newnham on Severn, Gloucestershire GL14 1DZ   01594 516304
Email:davidandpennyhill@btopenworld.com

Sharpham Partnership Ltd

Cheese and wine in tandem are the central products of the Sharpham Estate outside Totnes. Milk from the farm's Channel Island herd makes ultra-rich soft cheeses, whose main characteristic is rich, lingering, buttery taste.

(For the marriage of Sharpham wines and cheese see p.156)

Cheeses: Cow, Goat

P, V, OR

Sharpham: at around 1kg, the original Sharpham looks somewhat like a French Brie de Meaux, except that the outer mould is whiter. The rich curd that will eventually go runny has a suave texture and a clean, relatively mild taste. It's also made in 500g wheels and 250g squares.

Rustic: this young (about eight weeks) semi-hard cheese with a thin rind, has a fresh lactic taste and a creamy texture. It's also made in a chive-flavoured version.

Elmhirst: classed as a 'triple cream cheese', it can be eaten young (after two weeks) when it has an open texture and a fresh flavour. It becomes progressively smoother and more compact as it ages. Probably at its best at about six weeks, 1kg rounds and 250g squares.

Ticklemore: this is originally a Robin Congdon semi-hard goats' cheese that's now made at Sharpham. Under a rind that's marked by the colander in which it drains, it's a medium-flavoured cheese, quite moist, sometimes with eyes in the curd, growing more crumbly towards the centre.

Key suppliers: *Bath Fine Cheese Co., Paxton & Whitfield, Neal's Yard Dairy.*

Sharpham Estate, Totnes, South Devon TQ9 7UT
www.sharpham.com   01803 732600

Sleight Farm

Since she sold her flock of sheep, Mary Holbrook, a doyenne of Modern British cheesemakers only makes one goats' cheese regularly using milk from her own herd. Her Little Ryding is made by Wootton Organic Dairy (q.v.).

Cheeses: Goat

P, V

Tymsboro: shaped like a truncated pyramid, coated in ash, this could be classed as a fresh cheese, but it's made, as many French farmhouse cheeses are (hers is based on Valençay), to benefit from ripening. It's ready at around five weeks but would still be exciting at three months or more. It has a typical, mild goaty taste and a smooth texture.

Key suppliers: *Bath Fine Cheese Co., Country Cheeses, Neal's Yard Dairy.*

Sleight Farm, Timsbury, Bath, Avon BA3 1HN
          01761 470620

Smarts Traditional Gloucester Cheeses

Approaching eighty, Diana Smart is a doyenne of specialist cheesemaking. Her Single and Double Gloucesters reflect strong traditional values. She bought the business from one of the last remaining makers in the county at a time in life when most people would be thinking of retiring, equipped her dairy with Victorian presses and rapidly became expert.

Cheeses: Cow

U, V

Single Gloucester: 'If you can press your thumb into the rind and it springs back it's right.' Mrs Smart's 3.5kg semi-hard wheels are eaten at two to three months old when they are quite creamy in texture and lightly flavoured.

Double Gloucester: a more robust, drier cheese it's

ready at about six months when it has a deeper taste with a long finish.

Baby Single and Double Gloucesters: the two above cheeses are made as 1.5kg truckles.

Harefield: this unique hard cheese is nothing more than a Single Gloucester (except for a little extra heat in the curd during coagulation) aged for eighteen months, by which time it has a texture akin to grano and can be grated in the same way.

Key suppliers: *farmers' markets at Tewkesbury, Usk, Dursley, Lydney.*

Old Ley Court, Chapel Lane, Birdwood, Churcham, Gloucestershire GL2 8AR   01452 750225
Email:gloucester.cheese@farmersweekly.net

Sturts Farm (Sheiling Trust)

Sturt's Farm is a community run on biodynamic lines for people with learning difficulties and its cheese isn't generally sold to the public. It has its own cheesemaker producing small Cheddars with milk from a closed herd of dairy shorthorns.

Cheeses: Cow
U, V, O
Three Cross Road, West Moors, Ferndown, Dorset
BH22 0NF   01202 894292
www.sturtsfarm.com

Tamaracott Cheeses

Terri Rasmussen is an imaginative cheesemaker, who worked for Sue Proudfoot at Whalesborough before starting her own micro-dairy. Buying sheep's milk from a nearby herd of Friesland sheep, she is constantly innovating so the list below represents her core products.

Cheeses: Sheep
P, V
Little Mor: a small cider-washed rind cheese weighing about 100g, that can be eaten at four weeks and which will become almost runny by six weeks.

Hobbs Choice: hard sheep's-milk cheese, not aged like Pecorino, but ready to eat at about three months.

Lowen: 'Happy' in the Cornish language, a fresh cheese, eaten at about three weeks. Sizes range from individual portions to 500g.

Bowsy: Caerphilly style, but with sheep's milk, three to four weeks old, 1.5kg (sometimes available).

Baa Humbug: similar to Lancashire, but made with sheep's milk, best at three months old, 1.5kg (sometimes available).

Key suppliers: *Stephen Gunn's Cheese shop; farmers' markets at Bude and Lostwithiel.*

Tamar View, North Tamerton, Holsworthy, Devon
EX22 6RJ   01409 271439
tamaracott@gmail.com

Taw Valley Creamery

This sophisticated, modern Devonshire creamery makes Cheddar and other territorials.

Cheeses: Cow
P, V
Taw Valley Tasty: the aged Cheddar has some intentional crystallisation to give it extra crunch. Other Cheddars: mature, extra mature, mild.

Churnton: a successful, relatively new creamy textured hard cheese, it's marketed as a new territorial. It has a flavour similar to mainstream Cheddar but a softer, more open texture. It's sold both as mild and mature.

Combination cheeses: these flavoured cheeses include Cheddar and onion, Wensleydale and cranberry, Double Gloucester and chives.

Territorials: Double Gloucester, Cheshire, Leicester, Caerphilly, Wensleydale, Lancashire.

Key suppliers: *delicatessens*

Taw Valley Creamery, North Tawton,

Devon EX20 2DA   01837 880138

www.tawvalleycheese.co.uk

Ticklemore Cheese

Robin Congdon's first cheese, Beenleigh Blue, was an attempt at making Roquefort. In the twenty years or so since he started making it, the cheese has evolved and developed its own identity. It's less intense than the French cheese and rounder. Having made many different styles of cheese, he concentrates on blues these days. His Harbourne Blue, made with goats' milk is quite close in texture and edginess to Roquefort and the Devon Blue is a milder creamy cheese.

Cheeses: Cow, Sheep, Goat

P, V

Beenleigh Blue: this full-bodied sheep's-milk blue is creamy rather than hard. It's matured to develop a luscious, rounded flavour to which the blue veining gives an extra bite. About 3kg.

Harbourne Blue: the blue goats' cheese is more tangy than Beenleigh, the curd is white and more brittle and it has an almost sweet aroma. About 3kg.

Devon Blue: this rich, off-yellow cheese, made from Ayrshire milk, is foil-wrapped and matured for upwards of six months when it develops a texture akin to Beenleigh but with a lighter, more mellow flavour.

Key suppliers: *own shop, Country Cheeses, Neal's Yard Dairy, Paxton & Whitfield.*

I Ticklemore Street, Totnes,

Devon TQ9 5EJ   01803 732737

Times Past Cheese Dairy

e-mail: times.past@btopenworld.com
Web site: www.timespastcheesedairy.co.uk

A small, independent cheesemaking business with a dairy in Draycott, a village next to Cheddar, it supplies its own shop in the tourist centre and another in Weston-Super-Mare. It buys milk from the giant co-operative, Milk Link, but makes traditional cloth-bound rounds, territorials and some flavoured cheeses.

Cheeses: Cow

U, V

Cheddar: 27kg rounds are sold mature between twelve and fourteen months, or younger at eight months when they are of mild to medium strength. Stephen Webber, owner of Times Past, aims to produce cheeses with low acidity and no harshness in the aftertaste.

Red Leicester: this is a traditional millstone cheese (10kg, 2kg wheels), made in a similar way to Cheddar, coloured and sold younger.

Other territorials: Double Gloucester, Caerphilly, Cheshire.

Draycott Blue: this rich blue cheese with a smooth texture echoes old-fashioned, mature stilton.

Flavoured cheeses: garlic, pepper, sage and onion, whisky, cider and Marmite, etc.

Quarry House, Bridge Road, Bleadon,

Somerset BS24 0AU   01934 814204

www.timespastcheesedairy.co.uk

Toppenrose Dairy

The Lambrick family named its cheesemaking enterprise after the pedigree Friesian herd that grazes salty pastures near the Lizard. Only soft cheeses are made. They have a mellow taste, reflecting the excellent quality of the milk.

Cheeses: Cow

P, V

St Keverne Square: the square Brie-like cheese is similar in shape and size (250g) to Bath Soft Cheese, but more like the richer Cornish St Endelion in mouth-feel. It's also available smoked to produce a curious mould-ripened cheese.

Toppenrose Gold: this small round (100g) mould-ripened cheese is made like St Keverne, but with the addition of Jersey cream.

Key suppliers: *delicatessens, mainly in Cornwall.*
Trenance, St Keverne, Helstonm, Cornwall TR12 6QL
www.toppenrosedairy.co.uk   01326 280117

Tower Farms

A medium-sized member of the PDO West Country Farmhouse Cheese fraternity, Tower Farms makes both block and traditional cheeses.

Cheeses: Cow
P, V
Cheddar: the middle-of-the-range cheese, marketed at different stages of maturity is either sold locally or channelled into North Downs Dairy, through its Pilgrim's Choice brand, a rival to Dairy Crest's Cathedral City.

Key suppliers: *Own farm shop: farmers' markets at Taunton, Minehead, Bristol, Honiton.*

Deans Cross, Lydeard St Lawrence, Taunton, Somerset TA4 3QN   01984 667683
www.towerfarms.com

Vulscombe Cheese

Graham Townsend is one of the pioneering goats'-cheesemakers, starting off with his own animals, but since 1996 using bought-in milk from a small herd.

Although making fresh cheese, he takes great pains over the extended time that goes into making the cheese, up to sixty hours to coagulate the milk, plus twenty-four hours draining in cheese cloths and light weighting before moulding the cheeses.

Cheeses: Goat
P, V
Vulscombe: the round cheeses are naturally fermented without the use of either animal or vegetarian rennets. Lightly drained before shaping, they are full-fat rich and creamy.

Vulscombe log: drained a little more than the rounds, the size of Cornish butter logs, they are made as 250g 'sticks'. Best up to five weeks.

Vulscombe Herb: the farm grows up to twenty varieties of herbs and they may figure in the cheese in a variety of combinations, 170g, up to five weeks.

Vulscombe Peppercorn: peppercorns and fresh garlic flavour the basic fresh cheese, 170g, up to five weeks.

Vulscombe summer: fresh cheese flavoured with sun-dried tomatoes – nothing to do with summer, it's sold all year.

Key suppliers: *Crediton Market – 'for sentimental reasons'.*
Higher Vulscombe, Cruwys Morchard, Tiverton, Devon EX16 8NB   01884 252505

Westcombe Dairy

During the 1890s, a cheesemaker at Westcombe won a prize for the best cheese in the British Empire. Since then it has undergone changes of fortunes. It became a block Cheddar maker, shut down and then reopened in 1999 to produce traditional cloth-bound rounds. A member of the Slow Food Presidium elite, it makes unpasteurised Cheddar with animal rennet and specially selected starters.

Cheeses: Cow
U
Cheddar: each batch is different but farmer Richard

Calver believes the optimum age is about thirteen months. The texture is less friable than some aged Cheddars and the taste lingers on the palate. Westcombe Red: this annatto-dyed cheese, similar to Red Leicester, is sold at five months.

Key suppliers: *Neal's Yard Dairy and delicatessens.*

Lower Westcombe Farm, Evercreech, Shepton Mallet, Somerset BA4 6ER   01749 838031
Email.westcombe@farmhousecheesemaker.com

Westerly Cheeses
Cheeses: Cow
U, P, V
Curd Cheese: fresh.
May Cheese: fresh.
Westerly Cumin: flavour added.
Westerly Plain: Modern British, hard.

20 Pengilly Way, Hartland, Devon   01237 441057
vera@westerlycheeses.co.uk

Whalesborough Farm Foods
In an isolated corner of North Cornwall, Sue Proudfoot produces carefully crafted cheeses with milk, for the moment, bought from a single organic Ayrshire herd. This source is threatened by Milk Link, one member of the duopoly that controls liquid milk purchasing, whose policy would prevent the farmer supplying her. If this happens, she would have to rely on a Milk Link nominated supplier and the cheese would change.
Cheeses: Cow
P, V
Trelawney: a truckle-sized hard cheese, it's not over-pressed and retains moisture, rather like some American interpretations of Cheddar. The flavour is round, buttery with a subtle lemony tang.
Miss Muffet: the semi-soft cheese is made to a

recipe that's similar to Dutch Edam. It's springy with a gentle acidity allied to the taste of clean, rich milk. Keltic Gold: small drums (less than 500g) of Miss Muffet are turned into a washed-rind cheese that is both delicate and almost sweet-tasting.

Key suppliers: *Cornish farmers' markets, The Cheese Shop, Truro and delicatessens.*

Whalesborough Farm, Marhamchurch, Bude, Cornwall EX23 0JD   01288 361317
Email: seproudfoot@aol.com

Whitelake Cheeses
Peter Humphries was a cheesemaker for the Bath Soft Cheese Co. before starting out on his own, producing mainly goats' cheese on a farm near Shepton Mallet. He built his own dairy and works to his own recipes, producing interesting well-flavoured cheeses.
Cheeses: Cow, Goat
low temperature P, V
Whitelake Soft Goats' Cheese: Camembert-style cheese, 330g. At six weeks it still has a chalky thread in the centre, that by eight weeks has finished ripening to a buttery centre.
White Nancy and Rustic White Nancy: the same semi-soft cheese except that the rustic has a washed rind to give it a stronger flavour.
Rachel: a 2kg round, washed-curd cheese, still quite springy with a clean goaty flavour.
Morndew: the only cows' milk cheese from this dairy, it's similar to the White Nancy in style.
'Fetish': similar to Feta, but in cumin-flavoured olive oil (sometimes available).

Key suppliers: *Country Cheeses and Bath Fine Cheese Co; markets at Bath, Gloucester, Stroud and some London markets including Islington and Notting Hill.*

Bagborough Farm, Pylle, Shepton Mallet,
Somerset BA4 6SX   01749 830850
Email: roger@whitelake.co.uk

High Winds Farm, Higher Holton, Wincanton,
Somerset BA9 8AU   01963 33373
www.windyridgecheese.com

Wick Court Cheese

Farmer Johnathan Crump has one of the largest herds of Gloucester cattle in the county and turns its milk into excellent organic, unpasteurised cheeses. They take their name from a beautiful sevententh-century house occupied by the charity 'Farms for City Children' and although the young visitors don't get involved with cheesemaking they work on the farm and help with the livestock.

Cheeses: Cow

U, V, O

Single Gloucester: traditionally made Gloucester using part-skimmed milk.

Double Gloucester: wheels of aged Gloucester cheese, about 3.5kg with a firm texture and a buttery taste.

Key suppliers: *farmers' markets at Stroud.*

Wick Court, Arlingham, Gloucestershire GL2 7JJ
     01452 740117

Windyridge Cheese Ltd

This relatively new, still small rival to Ilchester Cheese, makes flavoured cheeses and hand-shapes grated cheese that is waxed in the shape of fruit.

Cheeses: Cow

P, V

Flavoured cheeses: from Bloody Mary to Afterburn (garlic and mixed bell peppers).

Hot Wheels: a selection of eight flavoured cheeses containing chilli peppers (1kg).

Dartboard: eight assorted flavoured cheeses using dried or freeze-dried flavourings (900g).

Key suppliers: *delicatessens, pubs and restaurants.*

Woolsery Cheese

Annette Lee used to have her own herd of goats when she lived in Devon. Since moving her dairy to a farm outside the picture postcard village of Cerne Abbas she has devoted herself full-time to making cheese.

Cheeses: Cow, Goat

P, V some O

Woolsery Goats' Cheese: the four-month-old hard cheese of truckle size has a subtle acidity, rounded flavour without too much 'goatiness' and lingering aftertaste. It's also available smoked.

Fiestsa: this is Feta cheese in all but name. It's less salty than the brined Feta in shops and Annette Lee also packs it in jars with herbs and olive oil.

Woolsery Soft: the spritzy soft goats' cheese in 100g pots is otherwise like the old-fashioned cream cheese that used to be made from soured milk.

Packwood: this four-month-old Cheddar is relatively moist with a buttery colour.

Meadowsweet: a full-fat semi-soft cows'-milk cheese.

Key suppliers: *farm shop, delicatessens, Neal's Yard Dairy.*

The Old Dairy, Up Sydling, Dorchester, Dorset
DT2 9PQ   01300 341991
www.woolserycheese.co.uk

Wootton Organic Dairy

Two Bartlett brothers run the sheep farm and their mother, Astrid, was their first cheesemaker. They make unpasteurised mainly mould-ripened sheep's-milk cheeses which were originally developed by Mary Holbrook of Sleight Farm when she kept sheep as well as goats.

Cheeses: Cow, Sheep

U, O, V

Little Ryding: this small seasonal – April to October – mould-ripened cheese (240g approx.) looks and eats like a Camembert fermier, except for the flavour of sheep's milk.

Big Ryding: as above but weighing about 1kg.

Shepherd's Crook: a narrower, deeper version of Little Ryding, it will mature a little more slowly and is less likely to flow when very ripe.

Old Burford: the Jersey milk equivalent of Little Ryding, the Bartletts make it to fill the seasonal gap when there is no sheep's-milk cheese.

Key suppliers: *Neal's Yard Dairy, Bath Fine Cheese Co., Country Cheeses.*

Sunnyside Farm, North Wootton, Shepton Mallett, Somerset BA4 4AQ   01749 890248

Email: 1bart@ukonline.co.uk

Wyke Farms

Originally a farmhouse cheesemaker, Wyke Farms has grown like Topsy to become the largest independent manufacturer in the country, producing thousands of tonnes each year.

Cheeses: Cow

P, V, some O

Simply Gorgeous: the mature block Cheddar is made, like all the cheeses, with a bulk starter unique to the company. This may give it a more rounded flavour than some other mass-produced factory cheeses.

TNT: this is an extra-aged cheese, fifteen to eighteen months old, often containing calcium lactate crystals that give an impression of crunchiness. The texture is starting to break down from hard and compact to crumbly.

Cheddars with differing levels of maturity sold as: Just Delicious, Rich and Creamy and So Mellow.

Truly Scrumptious: this aged Cheddar is made with a lower salt content.

Leskol: this slicing cheese, low in cholesterol, has been designed to supply the specific niche market that is concerned about the relationship between healthy eating and consumption of saturated animal fat.

Key suppliers: *delicatessens.*

White House Farm, Wyke Champflower, Bruton, Somerset BA10 0PU   01749 830312

www.wykefarms.com

Glossary

Cheese families

blue Any cheese that is intentionally veined with blue mould.

flavoured Flavoured cheeses are made in one of two ways. Either the flavouring, herbs, cranberries, mustard, etc., is added to the curd in the vat when the cheese is being made or it may be mixed with a finished cheese that is then reformed.

fresh It's a broad church including everything from freshly made goat's cheese to mozzarella that could be described as cooked. It can also refer to cheeses that may not reach their prime for a month or longer.

hard All cheeses, such as cheddar, that have been pressed are classed as hard.

mould-ripened This is a class of soft cheeses that mature under a white or mottled skin formed by the development of a mould, usually *Penicillium camdidum*.

natural rind If a fresh goat's or uncooked buffalo cheese is left in store it will eventually develop a mould-based rind on its own. Such cheeses are still quite rare in the West of England.

washed rind Sometimes these are soft, sometimes semi-soft. The cheeses are washed in a brine solution several times during the ripening process. They have a sticky exterior, often orange coloured.

semi-soft / semi-hard These terms can both be relatively confusing since they tend to be used to suit the understanding of whoever is using them For instance, both Cheddar and Stilton are sometimes called semi-hard because they aren't as hard as Parmesan. Cheeses that have a supple, bouncy texture may be relatively hard, but in England they are conventionally referred to as 'semi-soft'.

Traditional European Cheeses

Many of the new West Country cheeses have links to traditional European ones. The following list describes the more common ones.

Brie Mould-ripened cheese in the form of a flat disc that has been much imitated. There are several different sizes and styles weighing upwards of 750 grams, e.g. Brie de Meaux, Brie de Melun and Coulommiers.

Camembert Mould-ripened cheese weighing 250 grams, thicker than Brie.

Chèvre A general term in France for all goat's cheeses. They are made the same way and then shaped or ripened in an endless variety of ways, e.g. St Maure, Valençay, Picodon, Crottin.

Emmental Semi-skimmed, semi-hard, pressed cheese, made in very heavy wheels.

Feta Fresh, brined goat's or sheep's milk cheese from Greece.

Gorgonzola Italian blue cheese that may be sold young (dolcelatte) when it's more creamy or aged when it turns harder

Gouda A semi-hard Dutch cheese made with a cooked curd in the shape of a wheel with rounded edges.

Manchego Spanish sheep's milk hard cheese that can be aged from as little as two months to over two years and weighing 3–4 kilograms.

monastery cheeses This very catholic family of cheeses derive from monasteries where they were first made. They include 'smellies', washed rind cheeses such as Munster or Epoisses and springy semi-softs such as St Nectaire or Port-Salut.

Mozzarella Cooked buffalo milk cheese related to Provolone made from cow's milk. It forms strings when heated and drawn out.

Parmiggiano Reggiano Weighing up to 44 kilograms, aged from eighteen months upwards 'Parmesan' is a pressed hard cheese made from semi-skimmed milk.

pecorino Semi-hard to hard sheep's milk cheese in sizes up to 2 kilograms.

Tomme A family of cheeses semi-soft to semi-hard that may be made with goat's or cow's milk.

triple crème A semi-fresh cheese with a thin edible rind enriched with extra cream.

Vacherin A runny, silky, mould-ripened cheese.

General Cheesemaking Terms

acidity Sourness in the milk that is usually determined by the use of starters.

age It is only a rough guide to how a cheese will taste and should be related to other factors such as the type, size and condition of the cheese.

annatto The vegetable dye that colours cheeses, especially Double Gloucester, deep yellow to orangey-red.

back-slopping An old-fashioned technique for ripening milk that has been replaced by starters.

bacteria Living micro-organisms that are present in milk and essential to the development of flavour and texture.

bandage Binding rounds of cheddar with muslin or calico after coating them in melted lard is sometimes known as bandaging.

bloom The first development of moulds on the rind of a cheese.

blown A serious (fatal) fault in cheese cause by gas producing microbial action inside it.

blue A general term for veined cheese. It's usually the result of inoculation with *Penicillium roqueforti* mould of which there are many commercial strains.

breaking the curd The cheesemaker's term that describes a way of assessing when the curd is ready. If a finger is pushed into it, the curd breaks cleanly.

Brevibacterium linens A bacteria used in washed-rind cheeses that usually gives their surface a distinctive orange tinge.

brining Method used for salting cheeses either, as in the case of Caerphilly, before ripening, or as a part of the cheese's character in, for example, feta.

brucellosis an infectious disease caused by the bacteria of the genus *Brucella* that has been associated with consumption of raw milk products. It's rare.

bulk starter (pint starter) A traditional way of adding bacteria in a dilute solution to the fresh milk to ripen it favoured by some cheddar makers.

butterfat the proportion of fat, usually 2.5 per cent to 5.5 per cent found in whole milk.

casein The coagulated protein in milk.

cheese cloth Muslin or (now rarely) calico used to bind cheddar.

cheese iron A probe used to draw out a plug from a large, generally hard cheese in order to assess it.

churn Before milk was distributed in bulk tankers, it was kept and transported in large metal containers known as churns.

coagulation After rennet is added to the milk, it forms a gel or junket.

cook The term can be used in the commonly understood sense when curd is heated to a high temperature, or it may refer to gentle heating of the curd at low temperatures to extract whey.

cracked Sometimes during the maturing process the surface of a cheese may split.

culture As in 'starter culture': bacteria that are used to act on the milk so as to influence the flavour and texture of the finished cheese.

curd The solid part of milk made up of protein and fat.

cure A term that is sometimes used instead of 'mature' to describe the controlled aging of cheese – what the French call *affinage*.

cut Cutting the fresh curd, usually with specially designed horizontal or vertical blade knives, is a critical part of cheesemaking because it affects the manner in which the whey is released.

dairy The premises where cheese is made.

DVI (Direct Vat Inoculation) Starter concentrates added to milk.

drum A word descriptive of the shape of some cylinder-shaped cheeses.

E. coli A large family of bacteria that are associated in the public consciousness with food poisoning.

enzyme Protein that causes chemical reactions in cheese.

fat Along with protein, one of the two main constituents of milk solids.

ferment Cheese is fermented milk, as is also yoghurt, sour cream or crème fraîche.

follower A wooden slab, usually disc-shaped, that is placed between the cheese and the press during pressing.

friable Easily crumbled.

Geotrichum A yeast often used by cheesemakers working on mould-ripened cheese.

hoop Freshly formed curds are packed or ladled into hoops which will determine their eventual shape. Sometimes they are pressed while in the hoops.

humidity The humidity (and temperature) of the cheese store influences the way cheeses ripen.

ironing Boring a hole into a cheese and extracting a plug of it to test its quality.

junket A word not often used in cheesemaking these days that refers to the coagulated milk after renneting.

lactic 'milky'.

lactic acid Starter cultures bacteria consume sugars in milk (lactose) and produce lactic acid as a by-product.

lactose Sugar naturally occurring in milk.

lard Melted lard is painted on cheddar rounds and truckles before they are wrapped in cheese cloths.

linens See: *Brevibacterium linens*

Listeria The bacteria causes listeriosis and can occur in many foods. It generally has little effect on human health, but it can cause pregnant women to give birth prematurely or their babies to die in the womb. Raw milk soft cheeses are singled out as being high-risk products, because they have been known to carry the bacteria, but so do hot dogs.

macerate To soak cheese in oil and herbs in order to impregnate it with their flavours.

mesophilic A technical term used to describe kinds of starters linked to fresh cheese and Gouda.

mill The process of shredding freshly drained curd, common in cheddar making.

mite It's a tiny insect, barely visible to the naked eye, that lodges on the rind of maturing cheese and will eventually burrow its way into the cheese, if there are cracks in the rind.

mould (or mold) 1. Another word for hoop. 2. These microscopic growths of fungi are present in the atmosphere everywhere, but they can be both helpful and hurtful to the cheesemaking process.

mucor A black furry mould that spoils the appearance of mould-ripened cheese.

nutty A word that is often used when tasting cheddar to describe its taste when it has aged properly.

pasteurise Heat treatment of milk is carried out to destroy potentially harmful bacteria.

PDO Protected Denomination of Origin is an EC badge used to protect specific products including Cheddar.

Penicillium candidum A mould used in the making of brie-style cheeses.

Penicillium roquefortii A mould used in the making of blue cheeses.

peg mill A traditional mill that shreds curd during cheddar making.

PGI Protected Geographical Indication is another EU badge, which, for example, protects Dorset Blue Vinny.

phage A virus that attacks the bacteria in milk.

pitch (to) It describes the moment when the cheesemaker stops stirring the curd and lets it settle at the bottom of vat.

press (to) To compact cheese and extract residual whey by means of a cheese press.

raw A term generally used to describe untreated milk.

rennet The product of either animal or vegetable origin that coagulates milk.

ripen A stage of minutes or hours when the milk is allowed to undergo an increase in acidity due to the activity of cheese starter culture bacteria.

skimmed and semi-skimmed The description of milk from which part or all of the cream has been removed.

slipcoat An old word describing what happens when the outer rind of a cheese becomes detached from the maturing cheese underneath.

smear A process associated with washed rind cheeses where linens is smeared on the surface.

solids Protein and fat in milk.

sour Milk that has naturally curdled and become acidic.

Specialist Cheesemakers Association The body that represents independent craft cheesemaking in the UK.

starter A bacteria culture added to milk to develop acidity.

stir This is a critical part of the cheesemaking and its length and method have an important impact on how the cheese develops.

store The room where cheese is kept to mature it.

taints Off-flavours that may occur in cheese either because of the animal's diet or because of poor hygiene.

territorial Generic term for traditional English hard cheeses.

thermise A form of mild heat treatment that is sometimes used as a half-way house between unpasteurised and pasteurised milk.

thermophilic A kind of starter that's used with 'cooked' cheeses.

truckle The cylinder of cheese will normally be relatively small. It doesn't have to be of any special weight but, should weigh over 1.5 kilograms.

tuberculosis Bovine TB is a disease that increasingly causes concern to dairy farmers, some of whom pasteurise milk for fear of their herd contracting it and passing it down the food chain to humans.

ultrafiltration This is a modern process used by factory creameries to make 'creamcheese'.

unpasteurised The term refers to milk that hasn't been heat-treated.

vat The container in which cheese is made.

wash In some cheesemaking recipes the fresh curd is washed with water to remove any whey left on its surface.

wheel The shape associated with hard cheeses such as the Gloucesters.

whey The liquid part of milk after coagulation has taken place. It's a combination of water, milk, protein, lactose and minerals.

INDEX

Figures in italics indicate captions.

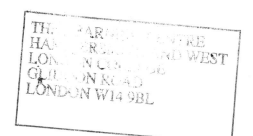